A PICTURE POSTCARD HISTORY OF U.S. AVIATION

by

Jack W. Lengenfelder

ALMAR PRESS
4105 Marietta Drive
Binghamton, New York 13903

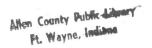
Library of Congress Cataloging-in-Publication Data

Legenfelder, Jack W., 1920-
    A picture postcard history of U.S. aviation / by Jack W.
Legenfelder. — 1st ed.
        p.   cm.
    Bibliography: p.
    ISBN 0-930256-19-0
    1. Aeronautics—United States—History.   2. Postcards—United
States.   I. Title.
    TL521.L36   1989
    629.13'00973—dc19
                                                              88-36433
                                                              CIP

Copyright © 1989 by ALMAR PRESS
              4105 Marietta Drive
              Binghamton, New York 13903

First Edition, First Printing . . . . June 1989

PRINTED IN THE UNITED STATES OF AMERICA

Dedication

To my wife Gloria for her encouragement
and to my children Barbara, Debra, John and Tim
for tolerating my overindulgence in things aeronautical.

Introduction

Virtually everyone who is blessed with an inquiring mind and leisure time eventually drifts into a hobby of some sort. Interests, aside from one's normal vocation which generates his or her income, can vary widely from building and operating model railroads to collecting highly valuable objects of art. Somewhere in between fall autograph collecting, stamp collecting and similar pastimes. Collecting has become an avocation of wide varieties: baseball cards, comic books, firearms, books, etc. When anyone becomes so immersed in the classification and organization of a treasured accumulation of objects that he/she creates a guidebook or a manual on the subject, it becomes clear that gathering almost anything can be a delightful undertaking. This enjoyment includes Postcards.

Jack Lengerfelder is and has been an enthusiastic advocate of light airplanes. As a result, it is not surprising that he began years ago to acquire Postcards oriented to aviation or Aviation Postcards. As we turn the pages of this unique book which traces the history of aviation from the era of the Wright Brothers and Glenn Curtiss through the aircraft of World War I, the era of barnstorming, World War II and up to modern aircraft—including military, air carrier and private—we must wonder (A) Who made the decision to create and circulate these historical artifacts and (B) What impelled Jack Lengenfelder to accumulate what are not necessarily the average collectible. Normally, the noncollector might consider Postcards as having the life expectancy of a moth. Yet some pictured in this book have outlasted the Biblical span of three score and ten years.

As an aviation enthusiast, I have found this unusual, perhaps unique book entrancing because of the wide scope of the aircraft which were at one time pictured on pieces of heavy paper designed to transmit personal messages by the least expensive means. The objects pictured in this book are "artifacts" in the true meaning of the term: they are Historical objects of Americana which tend to make the observer think about the past and contemplate the future.

Frank Kingston Smith
Vero Beach, Florida

Acknowledgements

I would like to thank the following individuals (listed in alphabetical order) for their contributions in helping to complete this book.

Harold Andrews, an early member in the American Aviation Historical Society, since 1960 a contributing Editor/Technical Advisor to Naval Aviation News, and author of numerous books and articles, for his comprehensive technical review of the manuscript.

Adrian C. Brooks, a corporate pilot and Postcard collecting colleague who has helped make Postcard collecting a most enjoyable hobby.

Dale Crites, an aviation pioneer and pilot of some of the early type Curtiss aircraft who provided information on the early Curtiss type aircraft.

William K. Evans, card collector and author who introduced me to the publisher.

Richard K. Farrell, airline and military pilot, for the generous use of his extensive aeronautical reference files.

George Hardie, Jr., antique aircraft authority and writer who provided information relative to the Wright Flyer III and Carillon Park.

George Townson, aviation writer and consultant for his numerous suggestions and encouragement.

John R. Turgyan, airline captain for the use of his large library of aviation literature.

Douglas Weiler, aviation writer for furnishing data on Hawthorn Hill, the home of Orville Wright.

My deep appreciation goes to each of the above people.

Jack Lengenfelder

Preface

As can be noted by the increasing number of shows, clubs, and publications related to the collecting of Postcards, the hobby has become a very popular pastime. There are Postcards available for almost any topic that one could imagine. For the past several years, this writer has found the collecting of Aviation Postcards to be the ideal complement to his older hobbies of aviation photography and the historical study of aircraft.

The opportunity to illustrate and describe these Postcards in a book proved to be a challenging and educational event. The arrangement of the Postcards is in chronological order within the book. I am certain that many important events in U.S. Aviation History have been omitted; either as a result of the fact that Postcards were not produced to denote the event, or I have not had the occasion to acquire the Postcards. Perhaps, this book will be the stimulus for some of these missing Postcards to be placed into circulation.

Although this book is not to be considered as a definitive history of U.S. Aviation, I hope this book will maintain the interest of the aspiring aviation historian and Postcard enthusiast and provide some new insights for the advanced historian.

The Postcard (or View as it is known to Postcard Collectors) is a snapshot in time. It may represent a building, street, home, scenic wonder, specific event, or any other subject involving human endeavor at the moment the picture was taken. In this book the scenes are of aircraft and they were selected to present a chronology of aircraft development and use.

The Postcard was initially used as an inexpensive and rapid means of communication between people. It provided space for a short written message and a photograph of a scene—frequently in color—that often was significant to the writer.

The communication written on the Postcard may or may not have been related to the scene. For example, the writer may have used a Postcard showing a picture of an aircraft that was important from a historical standpoint to inquire about the health of the recipient.

Many of these Postcards were collected for the message, history, and the photographic scene. Today, as a result of these collecting interests we have a very valuable source of information from a historical perspective. The Postcards show us aspects of the status of U.S. Aviation during specific time periods in the past.

As indicated above, any collection of these U.S. Aviation Postcards must be incomplete by the nature of the availability of the Views. Fortunately, people collected these Views and they were passed on in time to other members of the family and friends. However, all aircraft were not recorded on Postcards and all of the available Postcards were not saved.

As a result, this book represents a careful collection and selection of the available views representing specific aircraft in definite periods of time. In some instances, only one Postcard was available to this writer, although, I am certain that other Views must exist.

The descriptive captions for each view offer historical information combined with the comments of many interested people (see ACKNOWLEDGEMENTS) and this writer. No claim is made to originality or completeness in the captions.

A NOTE TO THE DELTIOLIGISTS:

To provide reference information for your collection of these Postcards, the following information was taken from each Postcard and added below each illustration.

Publisher: (Postcard No. and the name and address of the publisher)

Manufacturer: (Name and address)

Type: (Chrome, Black and White, Artist Color, Real Photo, Linen, etc.)

Postmark: (If the Postcard has been used, name of the Town, State, and Date)

Value Index: (A single letter based on the following code)
                 A = Very Rare
                 B = Rare
                 C = Fairly Rare
                 D = Scarce
                 E = Fairly Common
                 F = Common
                 G = Very Common

If any of these five items of information are not printed on either side of the Postcard then "NOT INDICATED" is shown below the illustration. There are listings that include all five items, some show one or more items, and some show none of the items.

Wright Bros, Original Plane - 1903, Kitty Hawk, N. C.

This historic first manned powered-flight with Mr. Orville Wright as the pilot (in the prone position at the center of the aircraft) was made, as planned, despite winds of 20 to 27 MPH on December 17, 1903. The famous photograph used for this postcard was taken by Mr. John T. Daniels of the Kill Devil Hills Life Saving Station. Mr. Wilbur Wright is standing at the right side of the photograph. In the right foreground near a shovel is a dry-battery coil box used for starting the engine.

The undercarriage of the aircraft consisted of two runners instead of wheels. The runners were ideal for landing on the soft sand of the beach. The takeoff was accomplished on a 60-foot single-rail starting track. The rail was made of four 2 X 4 X 15-foot pieces of wood covered with metal.

Publisher: Card No. ODK-2183, Hooper Bros., Elizabeth City, NC ■ Manufacturer: Curteich, Chicago, IL ■ Photograph: Smithsonian Institution ■ Type: Chrome ■ Postmark: Not Used ■ Value Index: F

The 605-pound aircraft was lifted onto a small roller-equipped truck on which it was propelled on the track. Forward motion was created when the aircraft engine was started and a restraining wire was released. The track is shown in the photograph below the aircraft. At the moment this photograph was taken, Wilbur has released his support of the wing tip as it moved along the rail and the aircraft was airborne. The aircraft was heavily damaged by a windstorm after the fourth flight on this date and was never flown again.

The original idea to transfer the flight operations to Kill Devil Hills, NC was based on the examination of many possible sites. The large sandy area was considered ideal for soft landings and the steady winds were ideal for their kite and glider flying. Much time had been lost at Kitty Hawk because the Wright brothers had misread the weather charts furnished to them prior to their locating there. Although the monthly wind averages appeared to be favorable, the day-to-day weather varied from a dead calm to wind speeds up to 45 miles per hour. These high wind speeds made the flight testing impossible.

The buildings shown in the photograph were con-

Publisher: Card No. P309618, Eastern National Park Monument Association ■ Manufacturer: Colorpicture, Boston, MA ■ Type: Chrome ■ Postmark: Kill Devil Hills, NC, December 17, 1973 ■ Value Index: F

structed at the site in 1953 as duplicates of the buildings used by the Wright Brothers as living quarters and aircraft hangar. The 10-ton granite boulder at the left edge of the photograph marks the actual point of takeoff for the four flights on December 17, 1903.

Publisher: Not Indicated ■ Manufacturer: Not Indicated ■ Type: Black and White ■ Postmark: Not Used ■ Value Index: E

Carillon Park was proposed in 1946 by Col. E.A. Deeds, Chairman, National Cash Register Company, Dayton, OH, as a permanent exhibition of early American Methods of transportation. The Wright Brothers were Dayton's most famous citizens and Col. Deeds contacted Mr. Orville Wright for an appropriate aircraft display. The first suggestion was a replica of the Kitty Hawk Machine of 1903. Mr. Wright later decided a restoration of the machine of 1905 would be a more suitable display. Fortunately, most of the machine was available for restoration.

This "Flyer" was flown from Huffman Prarie, a 90-acre pasture at Simms Station, approximately eight miles northeast of Dayton. This property was loaned to the Wright Brothers by their friend Mr. Torrence Huffman, a Dayton Banker. The land became the world's first airfield.

The 1905 "Flyer" has been referred to as the first practical airplane, as the Wright Brothers solved most of the problems of controlled flight using it. By 1908, they were making flights with a duration of more than 1 ½ hours. The Wright "Flyer" is also famous for making the first two flights with a passenger. Each of the Wright Brothers flew with their friend Mr. C.W. Furnas of Dayton. The two busts, shown in the photograph, on the balcony in front of the aircraft are of the Wright Brothers.

Hawthorne Hill, completed in 1914, was the home of Mr. Orville Wright, his Father, Bishop Milton Wright, and his Sister, Miss Katherine Wright until her marriage in 1926. Mr. Wilbur Wright never lived in the home as he passed away in 1912 as a result of Typhoid Fever.

Hawthorne Hill was named after the numerous Hawthorne trees on the site. The address was 901 Harman Avenue, Oakwood, OH, a suburb of Dayton. Hawthorne Hill was a symbol of the Wright success which included many unique features. One invention was a circular shower in the master bathroom. Mr. Orville Wright enjoyed a comfortable life entertaining many prominent guests includ-

Kodachrome by C. H. Ruth

Orville Wright Residence, Dayton, Ohio—84-D-17

Publisher: The J.T. Barlow Co. Publishing Division, Dayton, OH ■ Manufacturer: Dexter Press, Pearl River, NY ■ Type: Chrome ■ Postmark: Not Used ■ Value Index: E

ing Messrs. Alexander Graham Bell, Thomas Edison, Henry Ford, and Charles A. Lindbergh. After Mr. Orville Wright's death in 1948, the home was purchased by the National Cash Register Corporation. The company renovated the home, except for the library, which remained intact as it was at his death; the last book he was reading remained exactly where it had been placed. Although Hawthorne Hill is listed in the National Register of Historic Places, it is not open to the public.

39—Wright Memorial Beacon Kill Devil Hills, N. C.

WILBUR WRIGHT ORVILLE WRIGHT

Publisher: Card No. 3C-H142, Hooper Bros., Elizabeth City, NC ■ Manufacturer: Curteich, Chicago, IL ■ Type: Linen ■ Postmark: Not Used ■ Value Index: F

The site of the Wright Brothers first flight has been designated as the Wright Brothers National Memorial at Kill Devil Hills, NC. The site includes 425 acres with the main feature a 60-foot high gray granite monument built at an initial cost of $285,000. It was unveiled by the prominent flyer, Ms. Ruth Nichols on November 19, 1932. An observation platform and a beacon light are included at the top of the monument. The inscription states:

"In Commemoration of the conquest of air by the brothers Wilbur and Orville Wright. Conceived by genius. Achieved by dauntless resolution and unconquerable faith."

In 1929, before the monument was erected, work was begun to stabilize the 26 acre, 91-foot high shifting sand dune from which the Wright Brothers had flown. The sandy soil required the use of special grasses for seeding purposes. In later years, a 3000-foot landing strip and a visitors center were added to the site. Mr. Orville Wright is the only man to see a United States National Monument erected to him.

Publisher: Not Indicated ■ Manufacturer: Not Indicated ■ Type: Black and White ■ Postmark: Not Used
■ Value Index: E

GLENN CURTIS AND HIS BIPLANE

Publisher: Boston Philatelic Society ■ Manufacturer: Not Indicated ■ Type: Black and White
■ Postmark: Boston,MA, July 12, 1963 ■ Value Index: E

Although Mr. Orville Wright believed the original 1903 Wright "Flyer" should have been exhibited in the Smithsonian Institution, it was not given to the Smithsonian Institution. He had a lengthy dispute with the people in charge concerning the history covering the invention of the heavier-than-air aircraft and as a result decided not to display the Wright "Flyer" at the Smithsonian Institution. The dispute was based on the declaration of Mr. Samuel P. Langley as the inventor of heavier-than-air aircraft based on his flights of unmanned, steam-powered aircraft between 1896 and 1903.

In 1928, Mr. Orville Wright sent the airplane to the Science Museum at South Kensington near London, England, with the understanding that it would remain there until he made a written request for its return. In 1942, the dispute with the Smithsonian Institution was settled, and in 1943 he wrote to the Science Museum requesting return of the airplane when it could be safely returned following the end of World War II. The airplane was placed on display at the Smithsonian Institution on December 17, 1948, the 45th anniversary of the first flight.

The display has a plaque with the following text:

"The original Wright Brothers aeroplane, the world's first power driven heavier-than-air machine in which man made free, controlled and sustained flight. Invented and built by Wilbur and Orville Wright flown by them at Kitty Hawk, NC December 17, 1903. By original scientific research the Wright Brothers discovered the principles of human flight. As inventors, builders and flyers they further developed the aeroplane, taught men to fly, and opened the era of aviation."

In 1908, after the successful flights of the Wright Brothers (Orville in Dayton and Wilbur in Europe), Mr. Glenn H. Curtiss became prominent in the development of aircraft. As a rival of the Wright Brothers, he was accused by them of infringing on some of their patented aircraft features.

At an early age, Mr. Curtiss was obsessed with speed. He was racing bicycles when 14 years old. As the Wright Brothers, he operated a bicycle repair shop and began designing and developing engines and building motorcycles. In 1907, at Ormond Beach, FL, he drove a motorcycle at an unofficial world land speed record of 136 miles per hour. His highly efficient motorcycle engines became very popular and were adapted to aircraft use.

Mr. Curtis achieved recognition in aviation when he flew his "June Bug" in 1908. This flight occurred on July 4th, at Hammondsport, NY, at the Brook Farm Race Track. The occasion was to win the Scientific American Magazine $2,500 Silver Trophy for the first public flight in the United States over a One Kilometer Straight Course. Mr. Curtiss won the trophy, but he had problems in maneuvering his airplane in other than a straight line flight.

This photograph shows a later model of the Curtiss Biplane with a water-cooled engine and the ailerons installed at the edges of the wings on the struts between the wings. Mr. Curtiss is known for the designing of the Curtiss OX-5 Aircraft Engine and the Curtiss JN-4 Trainer.

VIEW FROM CURTISS AVIATION GROUNDS, HAMMONDSPORT, N. Y.

Publisher: Card No. A56798, H.M. Benner, Hammondsport, NY ■ Manufacturer: C.T. American Art, Chicago,IL
■ Type: Smooth or Pre-linen ■ Postmark: Not Used ■ Value Index: D

Publisher: H.M. Benner, Hammondsport, NY ■ Manufacturer: Not Indicated ■ Type: Black and White
■ Postmark: Not Used ■ Value Index: D

Mr. Glen H. Curtiss, either by choice or by accident, built his aircraft facilities at water locations, Hammondsport, NY and San Diego, CA. As a result, his aircraft designs were inclined to be those that operate from water. The lack of land-based airfields may have been an important factor.

From 1912 to 1915, Mr. Curtiss built a large number of hydro-airplanes as flying boats, a configuration which he patented. They all used the same basic configuration, a single hull, single engine with a pusher-type propeller, and like the open pushers with the distinctive mounting of the ailerons at the rear interplane struts. The variations in the designs consisted of engine size, hull shape, and experimental aerodynamic rigging of the struts. One significant change in the standard design was made for an aircraft to be demonstrated in Great Britain. The ailerons were mounted at the trailing edge of the upper wing.

In 1911 and 1912, the U.S. Navy purchased several of these Curtiss hull-type aircraft equipped for Over Water and Land (OWL) operations. This modification required the inclusion of wheels into the hull for land and water operations. The performance of the OWL was not up to expectations. In 1916 and later, the U.S. Navy purchased a large number of Model "F" Flying Boats as the standard training aircraft for naval aviators.

The first Flying Boat (hull-type aircraft) in the U.S. was developed by Mr. Glenn H. Curtiss in 1912. In 1914, he constructed the flying boat "America". This twin engine pusher-type aircraft had an upper wing span of 76 feet and was the largest aircraft in the U.S.A. to date. Mr. Curtiss planned to use this aircraft as an entry to win the $50,000 prize offered for the first Trans-Atlantic Crossing by a heavier-than-air aircraft. The beginning of World War I cancelled this plan.

The "America" was designed by Mr. B.D. Thomas under the direction of Mr. Curtiss. Mr. Thomas had been with the Sopwith Company in Great Britain and later became the Chief Engineer of the Thomas More Aircraft Co., in the U.S. $25,000 was contributed by Mr. Rodman Wanamaker and the aircraft became known as the "Curtiss—Wanamaker-America".

The "America" had excellent flight characteristics from the outset except, it could not lift the weight of fuel required for a Transatlantic flight. Many changes were made to the hull design and at one point in the design changes, a third engine with a tractor propeller was added to the top wing. The third-engine design was abandoned when the added weight of the engine required an excessive weight in additional fuel.

At the beginning of World War I, Great Britain purchased the "America" and 20 similar aircraft, known as the Curtiss Model H-4 and used them for coastal patrol.

Publisher: Southard & Associates ■ Manufacturer: Henry McGrew Printing Inc., Kansas City, MO
■ Type: Chrome ■ Postmark: Not Used ■ Value Index: D

The 1911 Curtiss Pusher "Kaminski's Sweetheart", shown in this photograph, is probably the oldest airworthy aircraft in the U.S.A. Mr. John G. Kaminski, born in Milwaukee, WI in 1893, was an early flying enthusiast. He learned to fly at the Curtiss Flight School in San Diego, CA on the site of the present North Island Naval Air Station. He was awarded Pilot License No. 121 on May 8, 1912 to become the first licensed pilot from Wisconsin. He immediately purchased this airplane and joined the Curtiss Exhibition Company performing with wellknown flyers including Mr. Lincoln Beachey. In 1916, Mr. Kaminski become a military flight instructor at Mineola, Long Island,NY. In 1917, he joined the Army Air Service and served in Panama throughout World War I. He gave up flying after the War because of failing eyesight, and worked for the U.S. Postal Service. He died in 1960. This aircraft was arranged with the pilot seat in front of the 90 HP Curtiss OX-5, V8 water-cooled engine. The aircraft was steered by moving the rudder with a steering wheel and tilting the wings by moving the ailerons using a shoulder rig. The engine throttle was operated by a pedal with the right foot.

In 1962, the Kaminski Curtiss Pusher was discovered in a barn near Waukesha, WI. It was acquired by Mr. Dale Crites who restored and flew the airplane in 1966. Dale and his twin brother Dean are aviation pioneers. The 81-year old twins have been flying for 63 years. They founded the Waukesha County Airport, now named in their honor and they continue to fly. Dale demonstrated this aircraft at many air shows before donating it to the Experimental Aircraft Association(EAA) Museum at Oshkosh, WI. One of these flights is shown in the photograph taken at the 1969 EAA Air Show at the Waukesha County Airport. In l974, the Crite Brothers constructed a replica of the Kaminski Curtiss and flew it at air shows until September 1987. On November 20, 1987, it was put on display in the Milwaukee Airport's Gallery of Flight Museum.

273 Hydro-Aeroplane out for a flight along the Ocean Front, Atlantic City, N. J.

In late 1916, The Curtiss Company produced the modernized "MF" boat. The "MF" was generally a larger and more refined version of the basic "F" model flying boat that had been in production for several years. Power for the "MF" series was the 100 HP Curtiss OXX engine. In the early 1920's, several surplus "MF" and similar "Seagull" civilian versions were used for sight-seeing flights from the beach-inlet at Atlantic City, NJ. The stripes on the rudder of the aircraft shown in the photograph would identify it as a military or exmilitary aircraft.

Publisher: P. Sander, Philadelphia & Atlantic City ■ Manufacturer: Not Indicated ■ Type: Pre-Linen ■ Postmark: Atlantic City, NJ, April 20, 1922 ■ Value Index: E

The civil variant of the Curtiss "MF" flying boat was known as the "Seagull". This four-seat aircraft was produced in limited quantities after World War I. A "Seagull" is shown in this photograph preparing for takeoff on a sight-seeing flight from Lake George, NY, the base of operations for a number of Curtiss Flying Boats.

175. THE START OF THE HYDROPLANE, LAKE GEORGE VILLAGE, N. Y.

Publisher: Not Indicated ■ Manufacturer: Not Indicated ■ Type: Pre-Linen ■ Postmark: Not Used ■ Value Index: D

With the scarcity of suitable landing fields, the operation of these larger aircraft from the water was the most practical approach. Most shore and lake resorts would boast of having at least one aircraft available for sight-seeing. Other than the military service, the use of these flying boats was restricted primarily to sight-seeing flights. They were not adaptable to airline or air-freight service because of their payload limits.

One of the most important outgrowths of the rapid development of the airplane was the "Aero Clubs". These clubs held aviation competitions near the larger cities. As an example, in August 1911, a nine-day event was held in Chicago,IL. With prize money of $100,000, this competition was one of the largest held to that date. Almost three million spectators attended, however, the event was marred by many accidents. Some of the accidents were attributed to the poor condition of the airfield which included pools of water and deep ruts in the mud. The accident shown in this photograph involved a Wright Brothers Biplane flown by Mr. Frank Coffyn, a member of the Wright

Brothers Exhibition Team. Mr. Coffyn was making a forced landing, with two passengers in his aircraft, when he collided with a Moisant Monoplane. Fortunately, no one was injured. The Moisant Monoplane, very similar in design to the Bleriot airplane, was designed by Mr. John Moisant. He was killed in an air crash on December 31, 1910.

Publisher: Not Indicated ■ Manufacturer: Not Indicated ■ Type: Black and White
■ Postmark: Denver, CO, September 26, 1911 ■ Value Index: E

A large part of the August 1911 aerial event in Chicago, IL was flown over Lake Michigan. Several of the aircraft were lost in the water. The early model Curtiss Hydroplane shown in this photograph was forced to land among the fleet of spectator boats that were anchored in the water offshore. The airplane apparently had damage to the forward control surfaces as a result of contact with one or more of the boats. Mr. St. Croix Johnson was one of the casualties when his monoplane exploded at approximately 1600 feet altitude and plunged into Lake Michigan, one mile offshore.

Publisher: Card No. 2205, V.O. Hammon Publishing Co., Chicago,IL ■ Manufacturer: Not Indicated
■ Type: Smooth or Pre-Linen ■ Postmark: Not Used ■ Value Index: F

WRIGHT ARMY PLANE, 1908-9. FIRST GOVERNMENT-OWNED PLANE IN THE WORLD. NOW IN U. S. NATIONAL MUSEUM, SMITHSONIAN INSTITUTION

Publisher: Not Indicated ■ Manufacturer: Curteich Co., Chicago, IL ■ Type: Black and White
■ Postmark: Not Used ■ Value Index: F

A Wright Flyer formally accepted by the U.S. Army on August 2, 1909, became the first U.S. Government-owned aircraft. The military version of the Wright Flyer was different from the civilian version because it had a newly designed 30 HP engine mounted in a vertical position and two seats with controls to permit the aircraft to carry a pilot and a student, or gunner, or observer. The first attempt to qualify the airplane for military operation in 1908 ended in a crash that killed Lt. Thomas Selfridge and injured Mr. Orville Wright. The crash was caused by a propeller becoming fouled in one of the bracing wires.

In July 1909, using a new and slightly refined aircraft, Mr. Orville Wright exceeded the duration tests by staying aloft for one hour and 12 minutes. Lt. Frank Lahm was also in the aircraft. Lt. Lahm later became one of the first officers selected for flight training. Mr. Wright, with Lt. Benjamin Foulois as a passenger, passed the speed test covering the prescribed course at an average speed of 42 MPH. The U.S. Government paid the Wright Brothers $30,000 for the airplane and flying instructions for two Army Pilots. The aircraft was operated by the U.S. Signal Corps mainly for observation purposes. On October 20, 1911, the aircraft was donated to the Smithsonian Institution when funds were appropriated for the Wright Flyer Model B.

1769. COLLEGE PARK, MD. WRIGHT BIPLANE LANDING ON GOV'T. AVIATION FIELD. JULY 29, 1911.

Publisher: Not Indicated ■ Manufacturer: Not Indicated ■ Type: Black and White ■ Postmark: Not Used ■ Value Index: D

The U.S. Army's first formal flying school was established at College Park, MD on April 11, 1911. Prior to this date, Mr. Wilbur Wright had given flight instructions to two officers, Lt. Frank Lahm and Lt. Frederick Humphreys in accordance with an established contract. By October 26, 1909, both officers had soloed. In 1911, the two officers were transferred to College Park to instruct personnel at the field and by the end of 1912, there were 17 trained U.S. Army Pilots.

Other interesting events that occurred at the College Park Base included the testing of Mr. Riley E. Scott's Bombsight and the experiments by Mr. Isaac N. Lewis with his air-cooled machine gun. The College Park Airfield has remained as the oldest continuously operated base in the U.S. and today it is maintained as a general aviation and sports flying center.

U. S. NAVY HYDRO-AEROPLANE

Publisher: American Colortype Co., Chicago, IL ■ Manufacturer: Not Indicated ■ Type: Pre-Linen ■ Postmark: Not Used ■ Value Index: E

The U.S. Naval Service began with the purchase of a Curtiss A-1 "Triad" Aircraft in 1911. The "Triad" was a basic Model D Curtiss Hydroplane modified to include a retractable main landing gear. This change produced the first successful amphibian aircraft. Three of these aircraft were built, but only one was acquired by the U.S. Navy. The eight-cylinder "Triad" could fly at 45 MPH and was priced at $5,500.

In 1912, the U.S. Navy purchased a Model E Curtiss Hydroplane and it became the first boat-hull aircraft, designated C-1 and later AB-1. The next four aircraft acquired by the U.S. Navy were one each of the Curtiss Model F Flying Boats in various hull refinements. The subsequent purchases by the U.S. Navy were all standard Model F Flying Boats for training purposes, as shown in this photograph, until late in World War I.

The training of our World War I aviators began with a two-to-three month ground course on a college campus. The second phase was primary flight training where they learned to fly these Curtis JN-4 biplanes called "Jennies". Until training facilities were built in the U.S., their advanced flying training was completed in Great Britain and France where more advanced types of aircraft were available, such as "Spads" and "Nieuports".

The "Jenny" was produced by seven companies in the United States and almost all of the aircraft remained in the U.S.A. for training. One version of the "Jenny" built in Canada was known as the "Canuck". The U.S. had only 55 pilots at the time America entered the war. At the Armistice, more than 10,000 pilots had been trained at home and 1675 in the overseas schools. Airfields for training had increased in number during this period from only 3 to 27 in the U.S. and 16 in France for advanced training. Camp Vail, shown in this photograph, located in Eastern New Jersey was not retained after World War I.

U. S. ARMY AEROPLANES.   GREETINGS FROM CAMP VAIL, N. J.

Publisher: Not Indicated ■ Manufacturer: W.H. Bechtel, Asbury Park, NJ ■ Type: Black and White ■ Postmark: Not Used ■ Value Index:E

The role of the airplane in warfare was gaining importance and new designs were appearing continuously. "Warfare in the Clouds" shown above, depicts aircraft types not normally used in combat and this scene could be a simulated or mock battle.

At the time of the U.S. entry into World War I, we were far behind our allies in design and production of military aircraft. To save time, a decision was made by the Aircraft Production Board to build aircraft of proven design. The DeHavilland DH-4 of Great Britain was chosen to be produced and nearly 4,900 were built in the U.S. However, by November 11, 1918, less than 200 were ready for service in the battle zone. These aircraft were powered by a V12 Liberty engine built by a group of automobile makers. The majority of U.S. pilots who were in combat during our participation in this conflict flew British-built Sopwith and S.E.5 or French Spad and Nieuport aircraft. The Americans lost 289 aircraft during their seven months of combat.

72040 WARFARE IN THE CLOUDS   (AUTHORIZED BY CENSOR)

Publisher: Card No. 72040, Detroit Publishing Co. ■ Manufacturer: Not Indicated ■ Type: Smooth or Pre-Linen ■ Postmark: Not Used ■ Value Index: E

MUSÉE DE L'ARMÉE   HOTEL DES INVALIDES

2   Le « VIEUX CHARLES », de l'Escadrille des CIGOGNES
Avion de chasse « Spad », du Capitaine GUYNEMER, avec lequel il a abattu 19 Avions ennemis

Publisher: E. LeDeley, Paris, France ■ Manufacturer: Not Indicated ■ Type: Black and White
■ Postmark: Not Used ■ Value Index: D

One of the most rugged of the Allied fighter aircraft was the French built SPAD, the name taken from the company, Societe Pour Aviation et Derives.

One of the three leaders of the SPAD firm was Louis Bleriot of cross-channel fame. Approximately 15,000 of the SPAD VII and the slightly larger SPAD XIII were built. With its completely enclosed water-cooled V8 engine, it climbed to 10,000 feet in eight minutes, and could dive faster than most any other aircraft. The SPAD was armed with Vickers machine guns mounted ahead of the cockpit and synchronized to fire between the propeller blades.

Mr. Georges Guynemer, France's second ranking ace was a frail and sickly youth who endured 26 months of combat. Guynemer's fate has never been established, but since he was subject to fainting it has been speculated that he may have crashed during one such spell. Twenty two of Guynermer's fifty-three victories were recorded while he flew his SPAD, which he had named "Vieus Charles" or "Old Charles". Two of America's top aces, Eddie Rickenbacker and Frank Luke also scored most of their victories in SPAD aircraft.

As World War I progressed, the U.S. hurriedly built a number of airfields for training purposes. Selfridge Field in Michigan was one of the largest and remained as one of the oldest active air stations. It was named after Lt. Thomas E. Selfridge, the first fatality from an aircraft crash. This accident in September 1908 occurred as Mr. Orville Wright, with Lt. Selfridge as a passenger, demonstrated an airplane for military acceptance.

While a member of the Aerial Experiment Association (a group of young engineers that included Mr. Glenn Curtiss), Lt. Selfridge designed a successful biplane in 1908. The aircraft was known as the "Red Wing" and was flown by Mr. F.W. Baldwin.

One of Uncle Sam's Army Aviation Schools.

Selfridge Field, Mt. Clemens, Mich.

Publisher: Underwood & Underwood No. 6569, Card No.680A Aeroplane Set - 6 designs ■ Manufacturer: Not Indicated
■ Type: Smooth or Pre-Linen ■ Postmark: Not Used ■ Value Index: D

Selfridge Field gained fame when it hosted a week-long airmeet in October 1922. Included in the activities was the International Pulitzer Trophy Speed Event. The event was a success and evolved into the annual National Air Races, begun during 1923 in St. Louis, MO. As a training field for World War I pilots, the aircraft shown in the photograph were the popular Curtiss JN-4 "Jenny". Between WWI and WWII, Selfridge Field was the home for squadrons of our latest pursuit aircraft.

In flight training, the discipline of formation flying was emphasized. This technique later proved important in both offensive and defensive situations. The British began formation flying as a defense for their reconnaissance aircraft and later their fighter aircraft adopted it for attacking as a team.

Major Jean DuPeuty, commander of a French air unit is credited with first using the three-dimension or echelon formation with the aircraft positioned to the side, above and behind the leader. This arrangement is still used in modern air maneuvers. Many of the prominent World War I aces were not receptive to formation flying, claimimg it restricted their individual types of

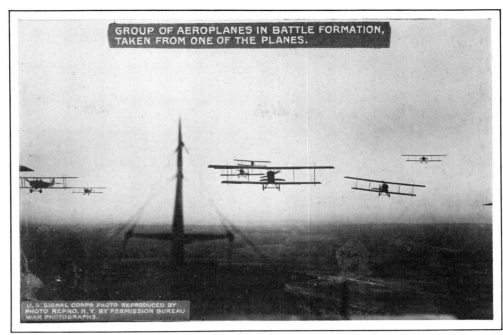

GROUP OF AEROPLANES IN BATTLE FORMATION, TAKEN FROM ONE OF THE PLANES.

U.S. SIGNAL CORPS PHOTO REPRODUCED BY PHOTO REPRO, N.Y. BY PERMISSION BUREAU WAR PHOTOGRAPHS.

Publisher: U.S. Signal Corps ■ Manufacturer: PhotoRepro., New York, NY ■ Type: Black and White
■ Postmark: Not Used ■ Value Index: D

dog fighting. The group of Curtiss "Jennies" shown in this photograph are flying in formation during a training fight.

Publisher: Card Nos. 80953 and JB-420, Old Rhinebeck Aerodrome, NY, Photo by L.W. Nelson.
■ Manufacturer: Not Indicated ■ Type: Chrome ■ Postmark: Not Used ■ Value Index: F

Many years after the end of World War I, the flavor of World War I flying is retained at Old Rhinebeck Aerodrome at Rhinebeck, NY where weekend shows during the summer feature the aircraft of World War I. This photograph shows an original British Sopwith "Snipe". It was considered the best fighter aircraft the Allies had in operation at the end of the war. Old Rhinebeck Aerodrome was founded and is operated by Mr. Cole Palen, who purchased the first six aircraft in his collection at an auction of World War I aircraft, in 1951, at Roosevelt Field, NY. By 1960, he was presenting once-a-month air shows performed with mostly volunteer help.

The Sopwith "Snipe" was one of the original six aircraft purchased. It was powered with a 230 HP Bentley Rotary Engine. It had been brought to the United States in 1927 for use in a motion picture film. The "Snipe" was used in the regular air shows from 1962 through 1966 when it was seriously damaged in a crash. It was later rebuilt and is on display in the museum at the Rhinebeck Aerodrome.

In addition to their flying shows, the Old Rhinebeck Aerodrome includes a museum with several buildings containing artifacts and nonflying aircraft of World War I.

While a large number of the Rhinebeck aircraft are originals, many unobtainable types have been reproduced by Mr. Cole Palen and his crew. In most cases, original

Publisher: Card No. 87623-C, Old Rhinebeck Aerodrome, NY. Photo by Kai Hulleberg. ■ Manufacturer: Dexter Color, 274 Madison Avenue, New York, NY ■ Type: Chrome ■ Postmark: Not Used ■ Value Index: F

drawings are used and original types of engines for the aircraft are installed if available. Where the original engines are not available, modern types of engines have been utilized. The collection also includes a large number of original aircraft from the period immediately following World War I. These aircraft are also used in the weekly airshows.

The aircraft shown in this photograph is not an original, as none of these World War I fighter planes exist. This Fokker DRI Triplane was built at the Old Rhinebeck Aerodrome from original drawings and uses a Gnome engine from the World War I period.

The German Fokker DRI was introduced in late 1917 to compete with Britain's Sopwith Triplane of similar design. In addition to the three wings, it had a short airfoil between the wheels. With a top speed of only 103 MPH and subject to structural failures, it remained in service for only a short period of time. While disliked by many German pilots, its good rate of climb and ability to maneuver tightly enabled some of the more experi-

Publisher: Old Rhinebeck Aerodrome, NY. Photo by E.J. Alexander ■ Manufacturer: Not Indicated ■ Type: Chrome ■ Postmark: Not Used ■ Value Index: F

enced pilots such as Baron Manfred von Richthofen to out-duel many foes.

Richthofen's last 21 of his 80 victories were scored while flying the Fokker DRI. He also lost his life in one of these aircraft; he flew many different DRI aircraft. Although Canadian Roy Brown has been credited by many with the victory of shooting down the Baron, Australian ground troops also claimed the credit of killing him and the dispute continues today.

1918 Nieuport 28   World War 1

Publisher: Ackerson, P.O. Box 23, Slate Hill, NY ■ Manufacturer: Not Indicated ■ Type: Chrome
■ Postmark: Not Used ■ Value Index: F

Another original World War I aircraft in the Old Rhinebeck Aerodrome airfleet is this French built Nieuport Model 28. Previous owners of this aircraft included the U.S. Navy and Paramount Studios. The production aircraft became available in 1918, and the Nieuport 28 was the first plane furnished to the American Fighter Squadrons. Capt. Eddie Rickenbacker scored some of his early victories in this type prior to their being replaced by the SPAD.

The Nieuport Model 28 followed the earlier Nieuport fighter aircraft (the models 23 and 24 were also used and had the same structural design as the model 17) which were equipped with a V type of interplane strut arrangement. The earlier Nieuport was a frail aircraft, and known for shedding it's wings if maneuvered too violently. The problem was corrected in the later models. Flying a newport, Mr. Douglas Campbell became the first American-trained pilot to score a confirmed combat victory, and later became the first official American Ace (with 5 victories) of the American-trained group.

The Barnstorming era began in the 1920s following the end of World War I. While some flyers engaged in regular airshow type performances with wing walkers and other stunts, the majority were content to sell passenger rides to the eager public. The most frequently used airplane for passenger rides was the war surplus Curtiss Model JN-4 "Jenny".

The Model JN-4 "Jenny" with the 150 HP Hispano-Suiza Engine which was used for some advanced training was preferred by the barnstormers over the JN-4D powered by the 90 HP Curtiss OX-5 engine, even though the OX-5 was more plentiful. The large number of war surplus "Jennies" and the availabil-

Publisher: Card No. 73384-C, Old Rhinebeck Aerodrome, NY. ■   Photo by Kai Hulleberg.
■ Manufacturer: Not Indicated ■ Type: Chrome ■ Postmark: Not Used ■ Value Index: F

ity of parts and engines made it the most practical plane for this purpose. The military stocks of "Jennies" and engines were not released by the government to civilian buyers until 1920. These "Jennies" were powered with the OX-5 engine. Later, other engines were included. In addition to civilian buyers, many "Jennies" were sold to companies for reconditioning and resale for civilian use. Later, unassembeled "Jennies" could be purchased for as little as $300, and engines for only $50. This photograph shows a "Jenny" at the Old Rhinebeck Aerodrome.

PAL-WAUKEE AIRPORT, INC.
A CENTURY OF PROGRESS

SIKORSKY   MODEL S-38

Pilot _____ Date

Publisher: Not Indicated ■ Manufacturer: Not Indicated ■ Type: Smooth ■ Postmark: Not Used
■ Vaue Index: D

Some of the more prominent pilots provided their passengers with postcards showing a photograph of their aircraft and their signature as momemtos of the flight. This passenger-hopping amphibian was the 10-seat Sikorsky S-38. Mr. Igor Sikorsky had built numerous aircraft in Russia. His first American aircraft built in 1924 was the S-29, a large biplane transport with two Liberty engines. The S-38 of 1928 was Sikorsky's first aircraft to be certified by the U.S. government.

The S-38 was developed primarily for use by Pan-American Airways on their Carribean Sea routes. Several of these same aircraft were operated by Inter-Island Airways of Hawaii for approximately 10 years. Either of the retractable wheels of the S-38 could be lowered independently as an aid to turning and maneuvering in the water.

In the late 1920s, passenger hopping continued to be a popular pasttime, and on most Sunday afternoons every local airfield and even some cow pastures would have at least one aircraft available for flights. Many of the aircraft were similar to this 1927 KR-31 or "Challenger C-Z".

This aircraft was built in 1927 by Kreider-Reisner Aircraft Company formed two years previously by Messrs. Amos H. Kreider and L.E. Reisner as an aircraft service company and Waco dealership in Hagerstown, MD. The KR-31 was a three-seat open cockpit biplane powered with the Curtiss OX-5, 90 HP water-cooled engine not too different from that year's Waco model. In 1928, a KR-31

FRIENDSHIP, D. W. AIRPORT, LE ROY, N. Y.

Publisher: Tichnor Quality Views ■ L Manufacturer: T.B. Cambridga, MA ■ Type: Smooth or Pre-Linen
■ Postmark: Not Used ■ Value Index: D

completed a grueling air race from New York at Los Angeles competing with most of the finest airplanes built in the U.S. In 1929, the Kreider-Reisner Company became a subsidiary of the Fairchild Aircraft Company, and later models were referred to as Fairchild KR-34C, etc.

This photograph shows a Curtiss Condor, Reg. No. NC726K at the Port Columbus, OH Airport while in airline service. The aircraft was later purchased by transatlantic flyer Mr. Clarence Chamberlin, along with other Condors for passenger hopping. Many of us had our first flights in one of these aircraft.

Publisher: Card No. 2A-H247, W. Ayres, 1047 Livingston Avenue, Columbus, OH ■ Manufacturer: Curt-Teich & Co. Inc., Chicago, IL ■ Type: Linen ■ Postmark: Indiana, PA, October 29, 1935 ■ Value Index: E

Although this aircraft appeared to be quite large for passenger hopping, the Condor, in the capable hands of an experienced pilot, as was Mr. Chamberlin, proved to be a profitable venture. In 1936 and 1937, he toured much of the eastern part of the country, often operating from rather small grass fields. The aircraft was eventually lost in a fire at Teterboro Airport in New Jersey. One of the operators of Port Columbus Airport during that time, Mr. Foster Lane, continues to maintain a building at the field and recently has been establishing a museum of antique aircraft.

DOMINGUEZ FIELD AVIATION GROUNDS. LOS ANGELES. CALIF. JANUARY. 1912

POSTMASTER GENERAL FRANK HITCHCOCK DELIVERING POUCH OF U. S. MAIL TO BE CARRIED FROM AVIATION FIELD TO POST-OFFICE. THIS POSTAL CARRIED IN THIS MANNER

Publisher: Not Indicated ■ Manufacturer: Not Indicated ■ Type: Black and White ■ Postmark: Los Angeles, CA. January 21, 1912 ■ Value Index: D

This photograph commemorates an important aviation event at Los Angeles, CA. The card is stamped (on the back side) "Official Postcard International Aviation Meet Jan. 20 to 28", and postmarked Los Angeles, CA Aviation Station Jan. 21, 1912. However, the photograph was actually taken at Garden City, Long Island, NY showing the delivery of the first sack of Official U.S. Airmail on September 23, 1911.

Postmaster General Frank Hitchcock is handing the sack of mail to Mr. Earle Ovington who was the first duly sworn United States Airmail Pilot. The aircraft used was a Bleriot type machine. This service between two Long Island terminals lasted only approximately one week. Thereafter, most large aviation meets featured Post Office sponsored airmail service flights. Regularly scheduled airmail service did not occur until 1918.

The first scheduled air-mail service by the Post Office Department began on May 15, 1918 between New York and Washington, DC. On July 1, 1919, the route between New York and Cleveland was opened with stops at Bellefonte, PA. The airfield shown in this photograph was used by the airmail service until 1926, in the area known as 'The Grave-

AERIAL MAIL STATION AND LANDING FIELD AT BELLEFONTE, NEAR STATE COLLEGE, PA.

Publisher: The Athletic Store, Inc., State College, PA ■ Manufacturer: The Albertype Co., Brooklyn, NY ■ Type: Sepia//Postmark: Fleming, PA, July 19, 1932 ■ Value Index: D

yard of Aviation'. The rough hills, bad weather, and lack of emergency landing fields were reasons for more aircraft accidents in this area than any other part of the country.

In 1920, the Bellefonte Airfield became one of the first radio-equipped fields in the U.S. By the mid-1920s, longer range aircraft had made this airfield obsolete. On a nearby mountain, in an appropriate ceremony, the Liberty engine of a mail plane that had crashed was dedicated as a memorial to all of the pilots in the airmail service who had died in the area.

519   PITCAIRN "MAILWING" USED BY N. A. T. FOR MAIL BETWEEN N.Y. & CHICAGO   Photo: National Air Transport, Inc.

Publisher: Unusual Photographs Reproductions Co., 19 Park Place, New York, NY ■ Manufacturer: Not Indicated ■ Type: Sepia ■ Postmark: Not Used ■ Value Index: B

In 1926, the Post Office Department began phasing out its airmail operations and awarding contracts to private operators. The last government mail flight was on August 31, 1927. Many operators found the Pitcairn Mailwing to be a durable aircraft for carrying the mail in all types of weather. Notable users were Pitcairn Aviation and subsequently Eastern Air Transport (New York to Atlanta) and National Air Transport (Chicago to Dallas).

The Pitcairn Mailwing was a single-seat biplane with a compartment ahead of the cockpit capable of holding 500 pounds of mail or cargo. The majority of these aircraft were powered with the Wright J-5, 220 HP air-cooled engine.

Some of the Mailwings were among the first in air transport to be equipped with radio.

Mail Autogiro flight from roof of Philadelphia Post Office   Philadelphia, Pa.

One of the most unusual airmail routes was that operated by Eastern Air Lines from the Camden, NJ Airport to the roof of the Philadelphia, PA Post Office. The Autogiro made five round trips per day, six days per week from July 1939 until July 1940.

The Autogiro shown in this photograph was a Kellett Model KD-1B, only one of which was built. During the period of operation, over 90 percent of the scheduled flights were completed. Each flight could carry 300 pounds of mail. The pilot, Mr. John M. Miller had been Kellett's test pilot. Mr. Miller remains an active pilot, flying his own twin engine airplane.

Publisher: K.F. Lutz, 441 N. 32nd Street, Philadelphia, PA ■ Manufacturer: Not Indicated
■ Type: Black and White ■ Postmark: Not Used ■ Value Index: D

We can safely say the most widely recognized of all airplanes is Colonel Charles A. Lindbergh's "Spirit of St. Louis". In this photograph, it is admired by some of many people who came to greet him in France after his historic flight. The aircraft was designed and built in only two months by the Ryan Company of San Diego, CA. This urgency was requested when Colonel Lindberg learned that he could not obtain the Bellanca aircraft that he had wanted to use for his flight.

Colonel Lindbergh's aircraft was derived from Ryan's open cockpit, parasol wing M-2 mailplane. It was a new design, a high-wing monoplane, with fuel tanks located inside the

LINDBERGH

Publisher: A.N. Paris ■ Manufacturer: Not indicated ■ Type: Sepia ■ Postmark: Not Used ■ Value Index: D

aircraft under the wing and an enclosed pilot's cabin behind the tanks in place of the usual open cockpit. These changes eliminated a windshield for forward vision and the pilot had to rely on a forward-looking periscope, except for a side window. Other changes, including 10 feet of extended wing span, were made to provide the necessary long-range performance.

The instrument panel contained all of the equipment commonly in use at the time with one exception. There was an Earth Inductor Compass. The wind-driven generator for this instrument can be seen mounted on top of the rear end of the fuselage. Colonel Lindberg had the first model of this device only recently invented by Mr. Maurice M. Titterington. This compass was credited with enabling Colonel Lindbergh to reach the Irish Coast only three miles from the planned location. The "Spirit of St. Louis" is on display at the National Air and Space Museum, Washington, DC.

The popularity gained by Colonel Charles A. Lindbergh from his famous flight resulted in his becoming involved in many other aviation activities such as flying the delegates of the Sixth Pan-American Conference at Havana, Cuba on sightseeing trips.

The Fokker F-7A Trimotor aircraft shown in this photograph was operated by Pan-American Airways on their Key West to Havana Route begun in 1927.

The Fokker Aircraft Corporation with plants at Teterboro, NJ was founded by Dutch Aviation Engineer Anthony Fokker. The crash of a later model F-10A Fokker Trimotor in which Notre Dame Football Coach Knute Rockne

Publisher: Pan-American Airways Inc. ■ Manufacturer: Capote & Diez (Barnet 68) Havana, Cuba ■ Type: Black and White ■ Postmark: Not Used ■ Value Index: D

was killed led to the withdrawal of the aircraft from airline service. Its all wood cantilever wing failed in flight, although the actual causes of the failure could not be determined.

Publisher: Pan-American, Artist: John T. McCoy ■ Manufacturer: Not Indicated ■ Type: Artist Color ■ Postmark: Not Used ■ Value Index: F

Colonel Charles A. Lindbergh is shown arriving in the Canal Zone on February 6, 1929 with the first airmail flight from Miami, FL. The aircraft is a Pan-American Sikorsky S-38. Colonel Lindbergh was a technical adviser and good-will ambassador for Pan-American Airways at this time. The S-38 aircraft was soon proven to be too small for the long over-

water routes. He worked closely with the Sikorsky Company to develop a larger aircraft as a replacement. The result was the S-40 "Clipper" four-engine amphibian carrying 40 passengers. This postcard shows a reproduction of one painting in a series of "Historic First Flights" by Mr. John T. McCoy for Pan-American Airways.

Charles and Anne Lindbergh on record flight

Colonel Lindbergh and his wife, Anne Morrow Lindbergh set a transcontinental speed record in this Lockheed "Sirius" aircraft on April 20, 1930. They flew from Los Angeles to New York in 14 hours and 23 minutes flying time. This aircraft, later equipped with pontoons, was used by the Lindbergh's on their survey flight to the Orient.

Colonel Lindbergh purchased the first Lookheed "Sirius" aircraft after having given the designer his ideas and some rough notes as to what he would consider as his ideal aircraft. The original design had open cockpits. The design was later modified at the request of Mrs. Lindbergh to have sliding canopies over the cock-

Publisher: Roy Votaw, Honor Pioneers 23-D ■ Manufacturer: Not Indicated ■ Type: Black and White ■ Postmark: Not Used ■ Value Index: F

pits. The aircraft is now displayed with the "Spirit of St. Louis" in the National Air and Space Museum at the Smithsonian Institution. After their 1931 survey flight to China, the Lindbergh's made a similar trip across the North Atlantic around Europe and returned across the South Atlantic. During the trip, the airplane was named "Tingmissartoq". In the Eskimo language, this word means "The one who flies like a big bird".

The wide expanse of smooth hard sand at Old Orchard Beach, ME made it an excellent jumping-off point for many Transatlantic flight attempts in the 1920s. The aircraft in the foreground of this photograph is a Bernard 191 "Yellow Bird".

Some of the more widely known attempts at Transatlantic crossings originating at Old Orchard Beach, ME included that of the single engine Fokker "Old Glory" with Messrs. Lloyd Bertaud, James Hill, and Philip Payne. The wreckage of this plane was located 600 miles off Newfoundland. Another attempted flight was that of Mrs. Francis Grayson with two male crew members in a Sikorsky S-38 aircraft. They were forced to turn

TRANS-ATLANTIC PLANES AT AIRPORT, OLD ORCHARD BEACH, MAINE   4567-29

Publisher: Card No. 4567-29 Not Indicated ■ Manufacturer: C.T. American Art Colored Co., Chicago,IL ■ Type: Smooth or Pre-Linen ■ Postmark: Not Used ■ Value Index: D

back after flying 500 miles at sea because of engine trouble.

Three Frenchmen, Messrs. Jean Assolant, Rene LeFevre, and Armeno Lotti took off on June 13, 1929 from Orchard Beach for Paris. They had to land on the coast of Spain. Their fuel consumption had been more than estimated caused by the extra weight of a stowaway. Twenty-two year old Mr. Arthur Schneider of Portland, ME had crawled inside the tail of the plane the night before the flight began.

43:—Capt. Harry Jones' Bellanca Plane, Old Orchard Beach, Maine.

A popular resident of Old Orchard Beach, ME was Captain Harry Jones. His personal aircraft was a Bellanca, similar to those used on numerous record flights. Prior to acquiring this aircraft, Mr. Jones had become well known for his barnstorming tours in a 1926 Stinson "Detroiter" Model SB-1 aircraft. This single-engine cabin bi-plane had seating for four persons. On these tours, the airplane was painted to advertise the H.P. Hazzard Shoe Company of Cardner, ME.

Publisher: Not Indicated ■ Manufacturer: Not Indicated ■ Type: Smooth or Pre-Linen ■ Postmark: Not Used ■ Value Index: E

This photograph shows the "Green Flash" aircraft at Old Orchard Beach, ME in 1929. In this Bellanca aircraft, Messrs. Roger Q. Williams and Lewis A. Yancey attempted a United States to Rome flight. As indicated in the following photograph, the flight was a failure. Designer Giuseppe Bellanca had built and flown his own aircraft in Italy in 1908. Considered an expert at airfoil design, the wing struts on most of Bellanca's aircraft were designed to have an airfoil cross section for additional lift.

The reliability of the Bellanca aircraft and their Wright engines made them eagerly sought for attempts at record flights. Bellanca's first manufactur-

Publisher: Not Indicated ■ Manufacturer: Not Indicated ■ Type: Black and White ■ Postmark: Old Orchard Beach, ME, May 3, 1929 ■ Value Index: B

ing facility was on Staten Island, NY. In 1928, with the backing of the Dupont family, he began operations at New Castle, DE.

A noteworthy flight by a Bellanca aircraft was the Transpacific trip of Messrs. Clyde Pangborn and High Herndon in the "Miss Veedol". They dropped the landing gear upon leaving Japan to save weight. Therefore, a belly landing was made at Wenatchee, WA where Pangborn's mother resided and he was familiar with the field. Taking off on October 4, 1931, this 4600 mile flight was completed in 41 hours and 13 minutes.

The remains of the Bellanca "Green Flash" at Old Orchard Beach, ME on June 13, 1929 after an unsuccessful take-off attempt by Messrs. Roger Williams and Lewis Yancey for a flight to Rome. They succeeded the following month in a similar aircraft; however, the aircraft made an unscheduled stop in Spain.

In a previous Transatlantic attempt in September 1928, Mr. Williams with Italian War Ace Cesare Sabelli had planned a flight to Rome. The take-off at Old Orchard Beach, ME was aborted when their Bellanca "Roma" would not gain sufficient altitude and was barely saved from going into the sea.

Publisher: Not Indicated ■ Manufacturer: Not Indicated ■ Type: Black and White ■ Postmark: Not Used ■ Value Index: B

A notable Transatlantic flight was that by Mr. Clarence Chamberlin in the Bellanca designed aircraft that Colonel Charles Lindbergh had sought to purchase for his flight to Paris. Leaving on June 4, 1927-barely two weeks after the Colonel Lindbergh flight—with Mr. Charles Levine the plane owner— the "Columbia" flew into Germany, landing only when its fuel supply was exhausted.

Publisher: Not Indicated ■ Manufacturer: Not Indicated ■ Type: Black and White ■ Postmark: Not Used ■ Value Index: B

This flight might have preceeded Colonel Lindberg's, had it not been for the bickering among the owners and crew about who would accompany Mr. Chamberlin. With this same airplane, "Columbia", Mr. Chamberlin and Mr. Bert Acosta had set an endurance record of more than 51 hours without refueling in early 1927.

After their successful Transatlantic flight, Messrs. Clarence Chamberlin and Charles Levine were treated royally on their tour of German cities such as their stop at Munich, Germany. A native of Denison, IO, Mr. Chamberlin was a Lieutenant in the Air Service during World War I, and prior to his record setting flights had been a test pilot for

Publisher: Not Indicated ■ Manufacturer: Not Indicated ■ Type: Black and White ■ Postmark: Not Used ■ Value Index: B

the Wright Company, a racing pilot, and barnstormer. Shortly after his return from Germany, on the S.S. Leviathan, he made a successful aircraft take-off from that ship. It was a test to prove the feasibility of using airplanes in conjunction with ships to speed up the transfer of mail and perhaps passengers as the ship neared port. In later life, Mr. Chamberlin was an aircraft designer and builder and also the operator of an aviation school.

The aircraft shown in this photograph was built in 1928 by the German Dornier Company. The DO-X was the largest airplane of its day. With a wing span of 157 feet and weighing 52 tons, it was originally powered by 12 Siemens-Halske engines which were later replaced with American Curtiss Conquerer engines. The normal seating arrange-

Publisher: Not Indicated ■ Manufacturer: Not Indicated ■ Type: Black and White ■ Postmark: Not Used ■ Value Index: D

ment was for 72 passengers. In October 1929, the aircraft carried 169 people to set a world record for the number of persons carried aloft in a single aircraft.

One fault of the aircraft was not being able to gain altitude when heavily loaded with fuel. The passenger carrying ability was reduced to practically zero for longer flights. It flew one 1400 mile leg of a flight from Germany at an altitude of only 30 feet. In two instances, it was forced to land and taxi for 60 miles on the water.

DO-X. ARRIVING IN NEW YORK   FAIRCHILD AERIAL SURVEYS INC. N.Y.C.

Leaving Switzerland on November 5, 1930, the DO-X began a leisurely trip to New York by way of South America. Troubled by many mechanical and other problems, the huge flying boat did not arrive in New York until August 27, 1931, completing a ten-month trip. It proved to be an impractical design because it was unable to lift a profitable payload, and was not placed into production. Two more were built for use by Italy; however, they were dismantled before being placed into service. For the return flight to Germany, the crew was reduced from 19 to 12, and with no payload the DO-X was barely able to carry sufficient fuel for the trip.

Publisher: Card No. 2009, Fairchild Aerial Surveys Inc., New York, NY ■ Manufacturer: Not Indicated
■ Type: Black and White ■ Postmark: Not Used ■ Value Index: B

In the early 1930s, setting intercity speed records had become the main activity of many former airmail and barnstorming pilots. The best known of this group was Mr. Frank Hawks, flying his Texaco Oil Company sponsored red and white "Travel Air Mystery Ship". By 1931, he had set approximately 200 city-to-city speed records in both North America and Europe. In this photograph, his aircraft is shown after landing at Calgary, Alberta, Canada, following a record flight from Edmonton, Alberta, Canada.

Some of Mr. Hawks' early speed records had been set in 1929 while flying a Lockheed "Vega", a six-passenger commercial airplane. Another feat for

Publisher: Calgary Photo Supply Co. ■ Manufacturer: Not Indicated ■ Type: Black and White
■ Postmark: Calgary, Alberta, Canada, October 11, 1930 ■ Value Index: A

which Mr. Hawks is known is being the first pilot to be towed from the Atlantic Coast to the Pacific Coast in a glider. He retired from speed flying in 1927 to devote his time to making flying safer. Ironically, he was killed while flying a Gwinn Aircar, an aircraft that was supposed to be exceptionally safe. The accident occurred as the plane struck high tension electrical wires. This accident cannot be considered the fault of the airplane.

A colorful attraction at most major aviation meets in the 1930s was Major Al Williams in his orange-colored Grumman "Gulfhawk". Major Williams is remembered for his scientific approach to his flying routine. As a result, these performances were beginning to be referred to as precision flying, rather than just daredevil stunting. Major Williams had been a baseball pitcher for the New York Giants. However, he was more attracted to flying, becoming a U.S. Navy pilot, and subsequently, a participant in the Pulitzer Trophy Speed Events. His precision flying routines began in the "Gulfhawk I" (the name Gulf was for his sponsor, the Gulf Oil Company) a Curtiss fighter-type biplane.

Publisher: E.A.A. Aviation Museum, Photo by Jim Thompson ■ Manufacturer: Not Indicated ■ Type: Chrome ■ Postmark: Not Used ■ Value Index: F

The "Gulfhawk II", as shown in the photograph, was a Grumman G-22, based on the Navy F3F. It is now displayed in the National Air and Space Museum in Washington, DC. A "Gulfhawk III" followed which was similar to the II except it was a two place aircraft. He used this aircraft mainly for cross-country flying and for carrying passengers. The "Gulfhawk IV", Major Williams' last aerobatic aircraft was basically a Grumman F8F, the Navy's late World War II "Bearcat" fighter.

AMELIA EARHART'S TRANSATLANTIC PLANE

Publisher: Ruth Murray Miller, Philadelphia, PA ■ Manufacturer: Not Indicated ■ Type: Blank and White ■ Postmark: Philadelphia, PA, January 14, 1937 ■ Value Index: D

The first solo Transatlantic flight by a woman was made by Amelia Earhart (AE) in May 1932 flying the single-engine Lockheed "Vega" monoplane shown in the photograph. The aircraft was displayed in the Franklin Institute in Philadelphia, PA. It has been relocated to the National Air and Space Museum, Washington, DC. In June 1928, AE had become the first woman to cross the Atlantic in an airplane. This flight was made in the Fokker Trimotor "Friendship" piloted by Mr. Wilmer Stultz and assisted by Mr. Louis Gordon. The flight left Trepassey Bay, Newfoundland and arrived in South Wales 20 hours and 40 minutes later. AE made another mark in aviation history on August 25, 1932 with her first nonstop transcontinental flight, by a woman, in 19 hours and 4 minutes.

Among her other accomplishments were the setting of an Autogiro altitude record of 18,415 feet on April 8, 1931 and the following month she became the first woman to fly an Autogiro from the Atlantic Coast to the Pacific Coast. Under the sleek and streamlined skin of AE's plane was wood construction. This construction was characteristic of all Lockheed "Vegas" except the last model DL-1 built in 1930 which had a fuselage of all metal construction.

AMELIA EARHART AND HER LOCKHEED VEGA

While attempting a round-the-world flight in 1937, Amelia Earhart (AE) and her navigator Fred Noonan disappeared as they approached Howland Island in the South Pacific. Many theories have been advanced as to the cause of their disappearance, none of which have been proven. The aircraft for this flight was a twin engine Lockheed "Electra". (The reference to "Vega" on this photograph is incorrect.)

Some individuals have speculated that AE and Mr. Noonan were on an espionage mission for the U.S. Government and were apprehended by the Japanese upon landing on a remote island in the Pacific Ocean. However, most serious researchers have

Publisher: Roy Votaw, Sebastopol, CA , Honor Pioneers-1 ■ Manufacturer: Not Indicated ■ Type: Black and White ■ Postmark: Not Used ■ Value Index: F

noted that there has been no evidence that supports this theory other than unsubstantiated recollections of various people. In 1967, the 30th anniversary of AE's disappearance, a similar round-the-world flight was made successfully by Miss Ann Pellegreno in the same type of aircraft.

CURTIS CONDOR

The Curtiss "Condor" aircraft was used by American and Eastern Airlines in the mid-1930s. It was the last of the biplane transports and the first to be capable of conversion to sleeping accommodations. One of these aircraft was acquired by Admiral Richard Byrd for his second Antarctic Expedition from 1933 to 1935. Normally the aircraft was

Publisher: Not Indicated ■ Manufacturer: Not Indicated ■ Type: Black and White ■ Postmark: Not Used ■ Value Index: D

equipped with a retractable landing gear. Byrd's aircraft, as shown in the photograph, had a fixed landing gear that could be adapted to skis or pontoons for the varied Antarctic conditions. While carrying the same name, it was actually a completely new design, and no relationship to the 1929-30 Curtiss "Condor" which had been developed from the B-2 Bomber.

1936 – VULTEE V1A SPECIAL

One of the largest single-engine aircraft at the time was the "Vultee" V-1A. Several were used by American Airlines from 1934 to 1938 as eight-passenger transports. The remaining example, shown in the photograph, was originally owned by Hearst Publications and is now part of the Shannon Air Museum in Fredericksburg, VA. It is a sister ship to the "Lady Peace" which was flown by Messrs. Richard Merrill and Harry Richman from New York to London and return in 1936. For this flight the wing was filled with 40,000 ping-pong balls to keep it afloat in the event of a water landing.

Publisher: Card No. 111569, Bill Buttram Photography, Fredericksburg, VA
■ Manufacturer: McGrew Color Graphics, Kansas City, MO ■ Type: Chrome ■ Postmark: Not Used ■ Value Index: F

The Lockheed Vega "Winnie Mae" twice made world circling flights in record time piloted by Mr. Wiley Post. The first flight was in June 1931 with Mr. Harold Gatty as navigator and the second flight in July 1933 was a solo trip. The aircraft shown in the photograph is the same as the "Winnie Mae" including the markings and registration number. However, the original aircraft is in the National Aerospace Museum in Washington, DC.

Mr. Post had lost an eye as the result of an accident on his job as an oilfield worker in Oaklahoma. He used the money from an insurance settlement to realize his lifelong ambition of learning to fly. One of his early flying jobs was

Publisher: E.A.A. Museum, Photo by Lee Fray ■ Manufacturer: Not Indicated ■ Type: Chrome
■ Postmark: Not Used ■ Value index: F

that of test pilot for the Lockheed Aircraft Company. As a result of this job, Mr. Post was able to meet Mr. F.J. Hall, an oil industrialist who purchased a Lockheed Vega and agreed to have Mr. Post make the record flight attempt in it. The "Winnie Mae" was named for the daughter of plane owner Mr.Hall.

In the summer of 1935, Wiley Post and his good friend, humorist Mr. Will Rogers, began a leisurely tour of Alaska in their pontoon equipped Lockheed "Orion-Explorer". On August 15, when taking off near Point Barrow, there was an engine failure. The resultant crash claimed the lives of both men.

The cause of the crash has been attributed to the

Publisher: Card No. 60908-D, Oklahoma Historical Society, Oklahoma City, OK ■ Manufacturer: Dexter Press, West Nyack, NY ■ Type: Chrome ■ Postmark: Not Used ■ Value Index: E

fact that Mr. Post had hurridly substituted extra-long pontoons for the aircraft, making the plane uncontrollable in the event of an engine failure. There were a number of additional airworthiness questions regarding this hybrid aircraft. In the photograph, Mr. Post is the man wearing an eye patch standing in the cockpit.

Ever since he had helped to build the "Spirit of St.Louis", Mr. Douglas F. Corrigan had dreamed of also flying the Atlantic. On July 18, 1938 he accomplished the feat, landing in Ireland after a 28-hour flight from New York. Claiming he was heading for California when taking off, he was always referred to as "Wrong-way Corrigan".

Publisher: W.J. Gray, Los Angeles, CA ■ Manufacturer: Not Indicated ■ Type: Black and White ■ Postmark: Not Used ■ Value Index: D

Mr. Corrigan's aircraft was a nine-year old Curtiss Robin, a single-engine monoplane of lightweight construction. He had purchased it as a used aircraft for $325. He completely overhauled it himself and added extra fuel tanks in the cabin similar to those used in Colonel Lindbergh's aircraft. Corrigan's autobiography, THAT'S MY STORY, was written without a ghost writer; he had fired the ghost writer. Corrigan also portrayed himself in the motion picture, "The Flying Irishman". It is reported that Mr. Corrigan continues to own the Transatlantic airplane at his Santa Ana, CA home.

Prior to the record flight described on this postcard, Mr. Howard Hughes had also set the world speed record of 353 MPH, and the fastest transcontinental flight from the Atlantic Coast to the Pacific Coast. In later years, he was to become known as the builder of the world's largest aircraft, the eight-engine "Spruce Goose" with a wingspan of 320 feet. The wooden flying boat only made one brief flight off the water before being put into storage for many years.

After considering the Douglas DC-1 and then a Sikorsky S-43-W for his around-the-world record attempt, Howard Hughes decided on a Lockheed Aircraft. The aircraft shown in the photograph was the

Publisher: Not Indicated ■ Manufacturer: Not Indicated ■ Type: Black and White ■ Postmark: Not Used ■ Value Index: D

model 14-N2 of the "Supra Electra" series. It was an all-metal, twin engined, low-winged monoplane with the latest instrumentation. Included was the Sperry Gyropilot and the latest equipment for radio navigation that kept the aircraft within six miles of its planned course. This twin-engined Lockheed aircraft was readily convertible for military use, and as World War II approached it was modified to become the well-known Lockheed "Hudson" bomber.

Publisher: Not Indicated ■ Manufacturer: Not Indicated ■ Type: Black and White ■ Postmark: Not Used ■ Value Index: A

This Travel-Air "Mystery Ship" set the design trend for future racing planes. It surpassed the best military planes in a feature race at the 1929 National Air Races at Cleveland, OH. The Travel-Air Manufacturing Corporation was organized in 1925 by Messrs. Clyde Cessna, Walter Beech, and Lloyd Stearman. Each of these men later departed from the organization to operate their own aircraft manufacturing company. Mr. Beech did not actually leave Travel-Air until Travel-Air became part of the Curtiss-Wright Corporation, and its identity was dropped to merge into Curtiss-Wright, St.Louis,. MO.

After placing second in the first Thompson Closed Course Race in 1930, the Travel-Airs were no longer able to compete with the speedier "Gee Bees" produced by the Grandville Brothers, and the new "Wedell-Williams Racers" which were very similar in design to the Travel-Airs.

100   CLEVELAND AIRPORT DURING AIR RACES

2A159

Publisher: Braun Art Publishing Co., Cleveland, OH ■ Manufacturer: C.T. American Art Colored, Chicago, IL
■ Type: Smooth or Pre-Linen ■ Postmark: Cleveland, OH, June 30, 1933 ■ Value Index: E

The annual National Air Races at Cleveland, OH and Los Angeles, CA were the major aviation event for the year during the 1930s. Closed-course races around pylons were conducted as well as cross-country races terminating at the airport. The crowded grandstands and parking areas, shown in this photograph, indicated popularity of this event.

The most important of the cross-country races was the event for the Bendix Aviation Corporation Trophy. This race was a speed event for any type of aircraft beginning at the West Coast and ending at Cleveland. The first of the Bendix Trophy races was run in 1931, leaving from the Burbank, CA Airport, and won by Mr. James Doolittle in a Laird "Super Solution" aircraft. His time for the flight to Cleveland was 9 hours and 10 minutes at a speed of 223 MPH; however, he continued on to Newark, New Jersey breaking the cross-country record previously held by Mr. Frank Hawks. He improved Mr. Hawks' record by more than one hour and collected an additional $2500 from the Bendix Corporation for the accomplishment.

The dwindling attendance at the National Air Races was probably caused by stretching the races to a 10-day event. In 1933, and again in 1936, the National Air Races were held in Los Angeles, CA as a four-day affair. In these years, the Bendix Race was run from New York to California and was won by Mr. Roscoe Turner in 1933 and Ms. Louise Thaden in 1936.

The stubby "Gee Bee" (named for the Granville Brothers) racing aircraft were an impressive part of the air racing activities for several years. Mr. Lowell Bayles, flying the Gee Bee Super Sportster 'Miss Springfield', shown in this photograph, won the important Thompson Trophy race on September 7, 1931. On December 5, 1931, he died in the crash of this plane while attempting to set a new speed record.

The Thompson Trophy Race was run on the last day of the annual National Air Races, sponsored by Cleveland's Thompson Products, Inc. The race was the most popular event in the meet. The first race at Chicago in 1930 was conducted over a five-mile course for 20 laps. In sub-

Publisher: Not Indicated ■ Manufacturer: Not Indicated ■ Type: Smooth or Pre-Linen ■ Postmark: Not Used ■ Value Index: B

sequent years, the distance varied from 60 miles in 1933 to 300 miles in 1938 and 1939. The initial race was won by Mr. Charles "Speed" Holman in a Laird "Solution" aircraft at a speed of 202 MPH. Gee Bee aircraft were the winners in 1931 with Mr. Bayles and again in 1932 with Mr. James "Jimmy" Doolittle as the pilot.

Very few of the original racing aircraft have survived and the building of several reproductions has been accomplished. One example is this reproduction of the "Miss Springfield" by Mr. Bill Turner of California. This "Gee Bee" is an authentic reproduction with the only deviations from the original aircraft being the installation of a tail wheel in place of the tail skid and the use of a radio. Both of these changes were made for safety reasons. One later alteration was the replacement of the wheel brakes with a more modern design braking system after a landing accident due to the failure of the original brakes.

Mr. Turner has logged more flying time in this

Publisher: E.A.A. Aviation Museum Foundation, Inc. ■ Manufacturer: Not Indicated ■ Type: Chrome ■ Postmark: Not Used ■ Value Index: F

"Gee Bee" than any of the pilots who flew the original aircraft. Mr. Turner has been involved in the building and flying of several other reproductions of racing aircraft, including the Brown B-2 "Miss Los Angeles" and the "Miles-Atwood Racer". His current project is a reproduction of the twin-engined DeHaviland "Comet", winner of the 1934 England to Australia race.

Colonel Roscoe Turner with the Thompson Trophy

NATIONAL AIR RACES Aug. 30 to Sept. 2 CLEVELAND

Lee Miles with the Louis W. Greve Trophy

The Cleveland National Air Races continued to be a Labor Day tradition until their interruption by World War II in 1939. This 1935 postcard provides an indication of the crowds in attendance and also shows the two previous winners for 1934. Although the purpose of the races has been debated, the races did serve as a proving ground for new ideas in design

Publisher: Not Indicated ■ Manufacturer: Not Indicated ■ Type: Black and White ■ Postmark: Not Used ■ Value Index: D

and construction that were later adopted by commercial aircraft builders. Included were designs such as the retractable landing gear.

For several years after the end of World War II, the air races were again conducted at Cleveland, but, they never regained the status or prestige of the earlier era. After the crash of an aircraft in a residential area, the races were discontinued indefinitely.

In the mid-1960s, the National Air Races were resumed. The Unlimited Class Closed Course Race of the Reno National Championship Air Races soon became the most popular national event. The majority of the unlimited class of racers are exmilitary aircraft such as this modified P-51 Mustang marked "Red Baron" using a Griffon Engine.

Publisher: Card No. ICS-108422, Aero Meridian, P.O. Box 2222, Carefree, AZ ■ Manufacturer: Not Indicated ■ Type: Chrome: ■ Postmark: Not Used ■ Value Index: F

In the unlimited class of racing, any type of modification is permitted to the aircraft subject to approval of a safety team. Most of the contestants use modifications comprised of a general cleanup of the airplane with fairings, eliminating any excess weight, and fine tuning the engine. However, some have been known to shorten the wings and reduce the size of the cockpit canopy to obtain extra speed. In recent years, the building of special aircraft specifically for unlimited class races has occurred for the first time since the early Cleveland Air Races.

One of the larger early aircraft of the U.S. Coast Guard Service was this Douglas "Dolphin" twin-engine Amphibian, acquired in 1931. Built in small numbers, a few were also used by the U.S. Army Air Force and the U.S. Navy. Several models of the Douglas "Dolphin" were built, differing mainly in the type of engine used and in the interior arrangement. Plush civilian versions were furnished to some wealthy sportsmen such as Messrs. Powell Crosley, Jr. and William E. Boeing of Boeing Aircraft Company.

An important design feature was the high mounting of the engines to provide ample propeller clearance and keep the blades away from the damaging water spray. The landing gear retracted to be clear of the water, but was not concealed and so it still contributed some drag on the airplane. One privately owned Douglas "Dolphin" is known to exist in the United States at this time.

Publisher: Not Indicated ■ Manufacturer: Not Indicated ■ Type: Real Photo
■ Postmark: U.S. Navy, December 27, 1944 ■ Value Index: D

Publisher: Card No. 31630, Photo by U.S. Coast Guard ■ Manufacturer: E.C. Kroop Co., Milwaukee, WI
■ Type: Linen ■ Postmark: Not Used ■ Value Index: D

This photo shows a typical Coast Guard Air Station of 1940. Three types of amphibious aircraft are shown: the 1935 Grumman JF-2 "Duck"; the Grumman JRF "Goose" in flight; and, a Douglas "Dolphin".

Only 15 of the Grumman JF-2 "Ducks" were produced for the U.S. Coast Guard. Many other models of this design were made, mostly for the U.S. Navy, and a few for Argentina. One model JF-2 was later transferred to the U.S. Navy and set an unofficial speed record for single-engined amphibians at 191 MPH in 1935. Several aircraft of this design have survived, most of them are in museums.

GRUMMAN "WIDGEON"

The Grumman model J4F-1 received by the U.S. Coast Guard in 1941 was the first military version of the civilian Grumman "Widgeon" amphibian. The two changes from the civilian model aircraft for military use were the addition of a hatch at the top of the hull for loading stretcher cases and the mechanism for carrying a single depth charge under the right wing. The J4F-1 was used mainly for rescue and patrol work, although in 1942 a Coast Guard J4F-1 sank the German Submarine U-166 off the coast of Louisiana.

There are numerous Grumman "Widgeons" in civilian use today.

Publisher: Not Indicated ■ Manufacturer: Not Indicated ■ Type: Black and White ■ Postmark: Not Used ■ Value Index: D

The majority of search and rescue operations conducted by the U.S. Coast Guard are now performed with HH-52A helicopters. Beginning in 1963, the Sikorsky HH-52A, shown in this photograph, has been used for these duties. This photograph was taken at the Coast Guard Training Center, Cape May, NJ.

The commercial version of this helicopter is known as Model S-62. The first flight was in 1958. It was the first amphibious helicopter with a flying boat hull, making it capable of operating from land, water, snow, and swampland. It is powered by a single General Electric turbine engine. The HH-52A helicopter can carry up to 3000 pounds either internally or slung beneath the fuselage.

Publisher: Not Indicated ■ Manufacturer: Not Indicated ■ Type: Chrome ■ Postmark: Not Used ■ Value Index: E

UNITED AIR LINES EIGHT TON, 14 PASSENGER-MAIL-EXPRESS
BOEING TRI-MOTOR PLANE AGAINST CHICAGO SKYLINE

The Boeing Model 80 aircraft are the only trimotor biplanes to be in service for U.S. airlines. The original Model 80 aircraft with a single Wasp Engines and seating for 12 people was initially used by the Boeing Air Transport (predecessor of United Airlines) in 1928 on their San Francisco to Chicago route. The later Model 80A aircraft shown in this photograph, pow-

Publisher: United Air Lines ■ Manufacturer: Not Indicated ■ Type: Real Photo ■ Postmark: Not Used ■ Value Index: A

ered by Hornet Engines could be arranged with seating for 14 or 18 passengers. They were operated on a 27-hour coast-to-coast schedule by United Airlines. All 80 series aircraft originally had single vertical tails and the 80As were modified with triple tails as shown in this photograph.

One aircraft, the 80B, of this model was built with open cockpits for the pilots. It was later modified to have an enclosed pilot compartment. The first use of air stewardesses was on these aircraft by United Airlines in 1930.

This photograph shows the first Fokker Model F-32 aircraft with the markings of Western Air Express. Two later F-32s were used by Western Air Express for their Los Angeles to San Francisco route beginning in April 1930. These aircraft had been ordered by Universal Airlines and Western Air Express. This first plane crashed while taking off on a test flight, and only Western put the aircraft in service using two of the seven that were built.

This large monoplane, with a wingspan of 99 feet, was powered by four engines, one tractor and one pusher engine under each wing. The tractor engines used two-blade propellers, the pusher engines had three-blade propellers of a smaller diameter to increase clearances. This aircraft was the largest and the last new commercial design built by the

FOKKER "F-32" TRANSPORT PLANE DUAL MOTOR - 30 PASSENGER   Photo: Fokker Aircraft Corp.

Publisher: Unusual Photographs Reproduction Company, 13 Park Place, New York, NY
■ Manufacturer: Not Indicated, Printed in Germany ■ Type: Sepia ■ Postmark: Not Used ■ Value Index: A

Fokker Aircraft Corporation at Hasbrouck Heights, NJ. In 1929, the Corporation had become an affiliate of General Motors Corporation, and in 1930 was reorganized as General Aviation Corporation with Fokker as a division. The aircraft was too expensive to operate, and a a result, four were scrapped without being sold.

The Curtiss "Kingbird", shown in this photograph, was a twin-engined, twin-tailed monoplane with seating for eight passengers. Approximately 30 of these aircraft were built and Eastern Airlines (then Eastern Air Transport) received approximately 15 of them. They were put in service by E.A.T. in December 1930 on portions of their New York to Miami route. They remained in service until 1935.

Southern Passengers Embarking Via Eastern Air

Publisher: Eastern Air Transport ■ Manufacturer: Not Indicated ■ Type: Linen ■ Postmark: Richmond, VA, October 4, 1931 ■ Value Index: A

The engines on the "Kingbird" were placed far forward and close together to minimize directional control problems in the event of a failure of one engine. After tests of early "Kingbirds" with 225-240 HP engines, the production aircraft were fitted with 300 HP engines.

Boarding 18 Passenger E.A.T. Airliner, Washington – New York

Publisher: Eastern Air Transport ■ Manufacturer: Not Indicated ■ Type: Sepia ■ Postmark: Newark, NJ, May 16, 1932 ■ Value Index: A

This photograph shows passengers posing for the photograph prior to boarding a Curtiss "Condor" airliner of Eastern Air Transport (now Eastern Airlines). Eastern began operating the "Condor" in December 1930 at the same time that they introduced the Curtiss Kingbird. Two "Condors" had been operated earlier that same year by Eastern Air Transport. The "Condor" was a huge aircraft with its double wings spanning over 91 feet compared to the 77-foot wingspan of the Ford Trimotor.

The "Condor" airliner was derived from the U.S. Army Curtiss B-2 bomber. The same general configuration was retained except for the removal of armament and gunner positions in the rear of the engine nacelles. It used the same 12-cylinder, liquid-cooled Curtiss Conqueror engines as the bomber aircraft. With the ability to carry 18 passengers in a soundproof and insulated cabin that included a lavatory, the "Condor" was considered the luxury airliner of the day. However, only six aircraft were built, all serving with Eastern Air Transport for a few years. Afterward, their main use was in the famous pilot Clarence Chamberlin's mid-1930s barnstorming operation.

The Early-Bird—famous first-plane in the Boston-New York daily fleet

A Ford Trimotor aircraft of American Airways is shown in the photograph on the Boston-New York route. This route is now flown by the Eastern Airlines Shuttle. The Ford Trimotor, commonly called the "Tin Goose" because of its all corrugated metal construction, became one of the most widely used and recognized of all aircraft used in commercial flying.

The first Model-AT flew in 1926, however, the Model 5-AT built during 1928-32 became the more widely used version. American Airways was formed in 1929 by the merger of five smaller airlines, and in 1934 was renamed American Airlines. Mr. Henry Ford became involved in commercial aviation in July 1925 when he purchased the Stout Metal Airplane Company from Mr. William B. Stout, a designer of metal aircraft.

Publisher: American Airways ■ Manufacturer: Lumitone Photo Print, New York, NY ■ Type: Pre-Linen ■ Postmark: Not Used ■ Value Index: B

Island Airlines was formed in 1953, when Mr. Ralph Dietrick's "Skytours" merged with Mr. Milton Hersberger's "Air Tours". The latter had been flying the Ford Trimotor aircraft since 1935. Considered the shortest airline in the world, the longest leg of its flight route was six miles. The airline operated from Port Clinton, OH and served the numerous islands in Lake Erie with passenger, mail, and freight service. As the last scheduled airline to use the Ford Trimotor on scheduled service, Island Airlines stopped using the "Tin Goose" in 1984 when the cost of insurance for the aircraft became prohibitive. The airline is still in business, using Cessna aircraft and a DeHaviland "Otter".

Publisher: Card No. ICS-72107-1, Kelly's Studio, 202 N. Potomac Street, Hagerstown, MD ■ Manufacturer: Not Indicated ■ Type: Chrome ■ Postmark: Not Used ■ Value Index: F

The surviving Ford Trimotor aircraft may be seen at the Ford Museum in Dearborn, MI, the Naval Air Museum in Pensacola, FL, and E.A.A. Museum, Oshkosh, WI, the Smithsonian Institute, and at the Hill Country Museum, Morgan Hill, CA.

UNITED AIR LINES "3-MILE-A-MINUTE" MULTI-MOTORED BOEING

First flown in February 1933, the Boeing aircraft Model 247, shown in this photograph, was considered the world's first truly modern airliner. The sleek all-metal design produced a three-mile-per-minute speed as advertised by United Airlines, who acquired all but one of the initial production output of 60 aircraft, plus additional improved 247Ds.

Publisher: United Air Lines ■ Manufacturer: Not Indicated ■ Type: Black and White ■ Postmark: Not Used ■ Value Index: E

Scheduled coast-to-coast flights were accomplished in 19 ½ hours.

The Boeing 247s were in airline service for less than a decade. While most were modernized to the 247D configuration, they were outclassed by the larger and faster Douglas airliners beginning in 1935. Some of the 247D aircraft saw several more years of service with smaller airlines after their replacement by United Airlines, beginning in 1936. A Boeing 247D placed third in the 1934 air race from London, England to Melbourne, Australia behind a special DeHaviland Comet Racer and a Douglas DC-2 aircraft.

PENNSYLVANIA AIRLINES' ALL METAL BOEING TRANSPORT

The Boeing 247D aircraft continued to have a useful life after being replaced by Douglas DC-3s. Pennsylvania Airlines merged with Central Airlines in November of 1936 to become Pennsylvania - Central Airlines. Several Boeing 247D aircraft that had been retired by United Airlines were purchased by Pennsylvania - Central for use on their routes from Washington, D.C. to the Great Lakes area. Pennsylvania - Central was renamed Capital Airlines in April 1948, and in June of 1961 was absorbed by United Airlines.

Publisher: Not Indicated ■ Manufacturer: Not Indicated ■ Type: Sepia ■ Postmark: Not Used ■ Value Index: B

The DC (for Douglas Commercial) line of aircraft was developed by Douglas Aircraft Company at the request of Transcontinental & Western Airline. The initial Model DC-1 and its successor the DC-2 were produced in small numbers, but the final version, the DC-3 (originally DST, for Douglas Sleeper Transport) soon became the favorite of most airlines. United Airlines who had pioneered the switch to the modern type transports with their Boeing 247s also had to acquire the better performing DC-3 to maintain a competetive position. The back of the postcard refers to this aircraft as their "Skylounge", and lists the following features: 14 deep cushioned swivel chairs; unusual visibility; real silver, china and linen; individual tables; hot meals; exceptionally quiet; air-conditioned; and, intraplane telephone.

Publisher: United Airlines ■ Manufacturer: Not Indicated ■ Type: Real Photo
■ Postmark: Seattle, WA, July 26, 1938 ■ Value Index: C

THROUGH WESTERN SKIES

Publisher: Western Air Lines ■ Manufacturer: Longshaw Card Co., Los Angeles, CA. ■ Type: Linen
■ Postmark: Not Used ■ Value Index: B

When Western Air Express became Western Airlines in April 1941, there were seven DC-3s in their fleet. The popularity of the Douglas DC-3 had continued to grow and at this time accounted for 80 percent of the U.S. Airline aircraft. Western also operated five Boeing 247D aircraft which had been released by United Airlines. Established in April 17, 1926, Western Airlines claimed to be the oldest existing airline as stated on the back of this postcard. Western was recently merged into Delta Airlines.

By 1939, with the exporting of large numbers of the Douglas DC-3, it was carrying 90 percent of the world's airline passengers. Allegheny was formerly All-American Aviation, an airmail service that used single-engine Stinson Reliant Aircraft equipped for dropping and picking up mail while in flight. Allegheny began using DC-3s after World War II.

Publisher: Allegheny Airlines ■ Manufacturer: L.B. Prince Co., Box 121, Arlington, VA ■ Type: Chrome ■ Postmark: Not Used ■ Value Index: D

Allegheny has become U.S. Air, and with the acquisition of several other airlines, has grown into one of the country's major airline carriers.

When Douglas DC-3 production was halted shortly after World War II, over 10,000 had been built. Most of these aircraft were built for the military, mainly as C-47s and with more than 50 other model designations. The military DC-3 or C-47 gained fame during World War II for flying the China-Burma-India route (the Hump) carrying war materials be-

Publisher: Northwest Airlines, Inc. ■ Manufacturer: Not Indicated ■ Type: Linen ■ Postmark: Seattle, WA, May 4, 1945 ■ Value Index: D

fore the larger C-46s and finally four-engine C-54s were available. They were used again as cargo haulers during the Berlin Airlift of 1948, although four-engine transports were the major types of aircraft that were used.

This photograph shows a DC-3 used by Northwest Airlines; acquired by Northwest Airlines in March 1939. Prior to that time, Northwest had used various models of Lockheed aircraft. In June 1946, Northwest was awarded a route to the Orient and thereafter was referred to as Northwest Orient Airlines.

THE INTERESTING WAY TO TRAVEL—EASTERN AIR LINES

Publisher: Eastern Air Lines ■ Manufacturer: Belgrave Press, Inc., New York, NY ■ Type: Sepia
■ Postmark: Not Used ■ Value Index: B

An interior view of an Eastern Airlines Douglas DC-2 airliner. Improvements over earlier aircraft include large individual windows with curtains, deeply upholstered and adjustable seats, a wide aisle, and overhead racks. Note the male steward employed by Eastern Airlines in December 1936.

Publisher: Card No. 57005, Fuson's Camera Shop, Grand Rapids, MI ■ Manufacturer: Dexter Press, Inc., West Nyack, NY
■ Type: Chrome ■ Postmark: Not Used ■ Value Index: E

This photograph is similar to a large number of "airport postcards". This scene at Kent County Airport, south of Grand Rapids, MI, depicts one of the small terminal buildings that were in use at many airports. These almost identical-appearing buildings were a commonsight. The Capital Airline markings on the Douglas DC-3 airliner, in the center of the photograph, indicate the time to be approximately 1950. Capital was previously designated Pennsylvania-Central and later was merged into United Airlines.

IWA Airline Hostess   IWA Color-foto

Publisher: Transcontinental and Western Air ■ Manufacturer: American Colourtype, Chicago, IL
■ Type: Chrome ■ Postmark: New York, NY, September 3, 1940 ■ Value Index: E

The idea of Airline Stewardesses was suggested to the Boeing Air Transport Company by Miss Ellen Church, a nurse at a San Franciso hospital. Receptive to the idea, the airline hired a group of eight nurses for this duty on their Boeing 80A Trimotors beginning in 1930. For a short time, Eastern Airlines tried the use of male stewards, but found that the public preferred the lady stewardesses.

The pay at that time for the stewardess positions was $125 per month for 100 hours of flying. Later, they were referred to as Air Hostesses. This photograph depicts the typical attire for the Air Hostesses of the 1940 period. The current Flight Attendants may be male or female, and the nurse requirement was deleted long ago.

The United Airlines Douglas Mainliners of the 1950s featured this well-equipped kitchenette. With their coast-to-coast flights requiring from 7-¼ hours (Model DC-7 aircraft) to 9-½ hours (Model DC-6 aircraft), there was ample time for the stewardesses to prepare and serve the many-course dinners described on the back of this postcard. With ap-

Publisher: United Air Lines ■ Manufacturer: Not Indicated ■ Type: Black and White ■ Postmark: Not Used ■ Value Index: D

proximately 60 passengers per plane, United Airlines estimated that it prepared 350,000 meals per year.

Modern airline catering services have taken much of the work out of meal preparation. The prepackaged meals require only heating and serving. Also, the greatly reduced times of many airline flights with less time aloft has reduced the meals to the serving of lesser meals and snacks.

The airline industry was revolutionized in the mid-1930s by the introduction of a number of new aircraft designs. One of these was the first twin-engine airplane produced by the Lockheed Aircraft Company. Their previous models had all been the single-engine "Vega", "Sirius", "Orion", etc. Although a rather small aircraft to be used as a twin-engine transport, with a wingspan of 55 feet, the Lockheed "Electra" had seating for 10 persons and a top speed of 210 MPH.

This aircraft was initially placed in service by Northwest Airlines in 1934. It was soon adopted by most U.S. airlines for their shorter routes, and also adopted by many foreign

Boarding Braniff Airways "Great Lakes To The Gulf" 10-passenger, twin-engined Lockheed Electra

Publisher: Braniff Airways ■ Manufacturer: Semco Color Press, Oklahoma City, OK ■ Type: Black and White ■ Postmark: Not Used ■ Value Index: D

airlines. Slightly more than 100 of these aircraft were built, the last one was completed in July 1941. Braniff Airways, described on this postcard, was renamed Braniff International in June 1948.

DOUGLAS DC-4
THE BIGGEST LAND TRANSPORTATION PLANE EVER BUILT IN THE UNITED STATES

Publisher: Not Indicated ■ Manufacturer: Not Indicated ■ Type: Real Photo ■ Postmark: Not Used ■ Value Index: B

The first Douglas Model DC-4 was this triple tailed, four-engine transport, of which only one was built. Partially funded by the five major U.S. airlines, it was test flown in June 1938. With a wingspan of 138 feet, it was the world's largest landplane at the time. It was the first of the larger model airliners to feature a nose wheel landing gear. The overall height of the tail assembly was reduced by using the three rudder design to permit entry into the hangers available at that time. After much test flying, it was sold to United Airlines in June 1939, who used it briefly for some experimental service. United Airlines became dissatisfied with the airplane, and it was sold to a Japanese airline where it was subsequently abandoned. After the smaller four-engined DC-4 was underway, the original DC-4 was referred to as the DC-4E for DC-4 Experimental.

LOCKHEED LODESTAR. A 14 passenger (crew of 3, total 17) all metal 2 engined high speed. Fastest Large Transport in regular A 'ne service in the world.

The largest and the last of the Lockheed series of twin-engine transports was the Model 18 "Lodestar". It carried 14 passengers at a cruising speed of approximately 230 MPH, the fastest airliner at the time. Midcontinental Airlines was the initial user of this aircraft in 1940.

This photograph shows the use of this aircraft by National Airlines. National

Publisher: Not Indicated ■ Manufacturer: Not Indicated ■ Type: Real Photo ■ Postmark: Not Used ■ Value Index: D

was the only major trunk airline never to have operated the Douglas DC-2 or DC-3. Many Model 18 "Lodestars" were militarized, some were used by the Air Corps as C-60 transports, and by the U.S. Navy as R50s. This design also served as a basis for the Vega "Ventura" Patrol Bomber.

The Curtiss Wright Model CW-20 aircraft was intended to replace the Douglas DC-3. Development of the CW-20 was begun in 1937 and it was test flown in March 1940. Designed to carry 36 passengers, it could lift twice the payload of the Douglas Model DC-3. The prototype, originally of large transport aircraft. It was put into service by British Overseas Airway Corporation in 1942.

As World War II was beginning, the entire production of this aircraft was taken over by the U.S. Military and all 3,182 aircraft that were built saw service, mostly in the Pacific Theatre of operations for flying the "Hump". The military designation was C-46, or "Commando". They were

Publisher: Not Indicated ■ Manufacturer: Not Indicated ■ Type: Black and White ■ Postmark: Not Used ■ Value Index: C

not to see civilian service until the end of World War II, when large numbers were converted for use by nonscheduled carriers and freight lines such as Slick Airways, the Flying Tiger Line, and Shamrock Airlines as shown in this photograph.

Publisher: Not Indicated ■ Manufacturer: Not Indicated ■ Type: Real Photo ■ Postmark: Not Used
■ Value Index: D

Publisher: Gorecke Photo, No. 22 ■ Manufacturer: Not Indicated ■ Type: Real Photo ■ Postmark: Not Used
■ Value Index: D

The first of Pan-American Airways' large "Clippers" were the Sikorsky Model S-40 amphibian. Though much larger than the Model S-38, and with four engines, it retained the awkward looking twin outrigger assembly for supporting the tail group. The appearance of this model had become very familiar although only three were built, namely, the "American", "Caribbean", and "Southern" Clippers. All three were used exclusively on Pan-Am's Transcaribbean routes. The inaugural flight was made on November 19, 1931 with Colonel Charles Lindbergh as the pilot. The aircraft had a wingspan of 114 feet, it could carry up to 45 passengers, but only at a speed of 110 MPH. It required a takeoff run of 20 seconds before lifting from the water.

As most of Pan-American's bases were located on the water, it was decided to remove the entire landing gear and operate the aircraft only as a flying boat. This change permitted an additional 1800 pounds of payload. The change was actually made in 1934 when all three aircraft were converted to the Model S-40A which also involved the replacement of the 575 HP engines with new supercharged Pratt & Whitney "Hornet" engines with 660 HP. In 1942, Pan-Am converted the cabin of the "Caribbean" Clipper into a 23 seat classroom for training British Royal Air Force navigation students.

The Sikorsky S-42 was the first true flying boat to be designed in the U.S. It was a radical departure from all of Sikorsky's previous amphibians with the twin-boom outriggers. Built especially for Pan-American Airways, it was flown on their first scheduled service to Argentina on August 15, 1934. Normal seating was for 32 passengers; however, the number of passengers could vary either more or less, depending on length of route being flown and amount of fuel required. The average cruising speed was 160 MPH.

Only three of the Model S-42 were built. In 1937, three Model S-42A and four Model S-42B aircraft were added to the fleet of Pan-Am. The principle changes in these models was the ability to convert the day-time interior to a 14-berth sleeper arrangement. Other changes included the switch to more efficient propellers and some changes around the engine nacelles and cowlings for better air flow.

The S-42 was used in 1935 to make the early survey flights to Hawaii, Midway, Guam, and Wake Island.

While on his second survey flight to New Zealand on January 11, 1938, Pan-Am's chief pilot Captain Edwin C., Musick and his seven-man crew were lost when their S-42B exploded as gasoline being jettisoned was ignited. A S-42 was also used to operate the first mail service from Seattle to Juneau, Alaska on June 20, 1940.

The China Clipper leaving San Francisco Bay

Publisher: Pan-American Airways ■ Manufacturer: Not Indicated ■ Type: Black and White
■ Postmark: Washington, DC., December 27, 1936 ■ Value Index: C

Yankee Clipper, one of Pan American Airways' Transatlantic Planes,
Entering its Hangar at the Baltimore Municipal Airport, Baltimore, Md.

Publisher: Calvert News Co., Baltimore, MD ■ Manufacturer: Tichnor Bros., Inc., Boston, MA ■ Type: Linen
■ Postmark: Not Used ■ Value Index: C

Probably the most well-known of all the Pan-American Clippers was the "China Clipper". This Model 130 Flying Boat, built by Martin Aircraft Company, with her sister ships "Philippine Clipper" and "Hawaii Clipper" had a wing-span of 130 feet and a cruising speed of approximately 150 MPH. The aircraft had a gross weight of 52,000 pounds, landings were not to be made at over 48,000 pounds so that the excess weight (usually fuel) had to be jettisoned. The design incorporated the use of short Sponsors or "Seawings" at the lower hull. These were for stability while maneuvering on the water in place of the earlier outer wing-mounted floats. They also contained fuel tanks and their airfoil shape contributed lift for the aircraft. With a cabin capable of accommodating up to 52 passengers, on longer flights it frequently carried as few as 14 with the necessary fuel on board and the balance of the payload made up of mail and cargo.

The first scheduled Transpacific mail service was flown by the "China Clipper" on November 22, 1935, with regular passenger service beginning one year later. The navigation officer on many of the "China Clipper" flights was Mr. Fred J. Noonan who was later to be Amelia Earhart's navigator on her ill-fated attempt to fly around the world. The careers of all three of these Clippers came to tragic endings. The "Hawaii Clipper" disappeared on a flight between Guam and Manila on July 28, 1938, the "Philippine Clipper" was lost on January 21, 1943 when it flew into high ground near Ukiah, CA during bad weather on its return from Hawaii while in Navy service, and the "China Clipper" sank after striking an object in the water at Trinidad on January 8, 1945. It had returned to Pan-American after being in Navy Service.

The last of the Pan-American Airways flying boats were the 12 Boeing Model 314 "Clippers". Of somewhat similar configuration to the previous Martin Model 130 aircraft, they were much heavier (42 tons) and larger (152 foot wing-span). The prototype was built with a single tail fin which proved inadequate in tests and was replaced with a twin rudder arrangement. This design was then changed to the final triple-rudder design. The Model 314 carried 34 passengers and cargo on Transatlantic flights, and as many as 74 passengers and crew of five on shorter flights. It had a cruising speed of 184 MPH. Among the major accomplishments of the Boeing 314 were its first scheduled mail flight across the Atlantic on May 20, 1939, and the first scheduled Transatlantic passenger flight on June 28, 1939. They were also used on Pan-Am's Transpacific routes to New Zealand and Singapore. A Boeing 314, the "Dixie Clipper" was used to fly President Franklin Roosevelt to the Casablanca Conference in January 1943.

This photograph shows the Baltimore terminus of the Transatlantic route from Poole, England. This route was also flown by the British Overseas Airways Corporation who had purchased three of the 314 aircraft from Pan-American. The "Yankee Clipper" in this photograph was the only Model 314 to be lost in a flying accident. The accident occurred on February 22, 1943, when a wing-tip struck the water as it banked for a landing approach at Lisbon, Portugal. One of the 15 survivors was singer Jane Froman, who was traveling with a U.S.O. Troupe. The severely injured Miss Froman was kept afloat by Fourth Officer John C. Burns whom she later married. The last "Clipper" flight by Pan-Am was on April 8, 1946. Some additional flights were attempted on nonscheduled airlines by unsuccessful operators such as Universal Airlines and American International Airways. The last aircraft was scrapped in late 1951.

The size of the crew varied from six members on the S-40 to ten on the Boeing 314 "Clippers". The basic flight crew would consist of pilot, co-pilot, radio operator, navigator, and flight mechanic. Other crew personnel included the purser and a varying number of cabin attendants. Each "Clipper" was equipped with dual sets of controls and instruments. Blind flying instruments had become quite reliable as had the Sperry Automatic Pilot. However, radio and navigation systems were not fully developed and required constant attention. Constant corrections were required, especially when the destinations were the tiny islands in the Pacific Ocean.

On the Bridge of a "Flying Clipper Ship"

Publisher: Pan-American Airways ■ Manufacturer: Not Indicated ■ Type: Black and White
■ Postmark: Not Used ■ Value Index: D

On the Martin Model 130 "China Clipper", the flight mechanic had a separate room in the pylon supporting the wing which contained controls for the engines, propellers, and fuel. On the largest "Clippers", the Boeing 314, the thickness of the wing was sufficient to allow passage through it by the flight mechanic to make adjustments to the engines while in flight.

AIRVIEW OF PAN AMERICAN AIRPORT, MIAMI   178

Publisher: Not Indicated ■ Manufacturer: Not Indicated ■ Type: Real Photo
■ Postmark: Miami Beach, FL, December 4, 1941 ■ Value Index: E

Built in the early 1930s, the Pan-American Airways elaborate terminal at Binner Key, Miami, FL was known as the world's largest air terminal, and as the "Gate-way between the Americas". Large crowds were attracted to the base to watch the big "Clippers" depart and arrive and be towed from the water by tractors.

Five types of "Clippers" may be seen in this photograph. Beginning top-center are a Sikorsky S-40 and S-42 near the hangars, moving clockwise, a Consolidated "Commodore" in the water. These lesser known of the flying boats were acquired by Pan-Am from New York, Rio, and Buenos Aires Lines who had operated them on a route along the East Coast of South America. In the lower left, in water another S-42, left center, on land, a Sikorsky S-43 (the two-engine "Mini-Clipper") and above it, on land, an older Sikorsky S-38, the two-engine design with the twin out-riggers.

CHALK'S INTERNATIONAL AIRLINES —— *Bimini, Bahamas* ——

Publisher: Chalk's International Airlines ■ Manufacturer: U.S. and Caribbean Promotions ■ Type: Chrome
■ Postmark: Bimini, Bahamas, February 21, 1978 ■ Value Index: E

Claiming to be the world's oldest airline, Chalk's International was founded in 1919 by Captain A.B. Chalk as Chalk's Flying Service. It has been operating since that date with amphibious aircraft between Miami, FL and the Bahamas. The Airline is currently using the Grumman "Mallard" Amphibian. This 1946 design is an enlarged development of the earlier Grumman "Goose" and "Widgeon". Intended for feeder airline use, most of the 59 aircraft that were produced went to wealthy sportsmen and large corporations including Mr. Henry Ford. The all-metal "Mallard" with a wingspan of 67 feet had seating for ten passengers and two pilots. Many of the aircraft continue in use with some being operated by the same owners for more than 25 years.

Another claim made by Chalk's International is that they have never had a fatality nor an injury to a passenger. Chalk's has also recently put into service the Grumman "Albatross", an amphibian of practically the same configuration as the "Mallard". It is slightly larger with a wingspan of 80 feet.

Catalina Airlines began operations in 1953 as the Avalon Air Transport. The name changed in 1963. The 21-mile route from Long Beach, CA to Catalina Island had previously been covered by United Airlines, who found it to be unprofitable for their Douglas DC-3s. During the summer months, as many as 70 round trips per day have been made. Their fleet consisted mainly of the Grumman "Goose" Amphibian. This aircraft was the forerunner of the slightly smaller Grumman "Widgeon". Both of these aircraft had been used by the military, primarily for patrol work. The "Goose" shown on this postcard has been modified; the fixed wing floats were converted to the retractable wing tips. This modification improved the passengers' vision, and enhanced the aircraft's performance.

Publisher: SceniKrome from Golden West, 700 W. Willow Street, Long Beach, CA
■ Manufacturer: H.S. Crocker Co., Inc., San Francisco, CA ■ Type: Chrome ■ Postmark: Not Used ■ Value Index: E

In 1957, Catalina Airlines also began operating the only remaining Sikorsky VS-44, originally operated by American Overseas Airlines. This aircraft was a four-engine, 47 passenger flying boat. Operations ended in 1959; however, a new carrier, Trans-Catalina is now serving the route.

GOODYEAR "SPUR" BLIMP—150 ft. long—48 ft. diam.—123,000 cu. ft. non-explosive helium.

Publisher: Not Indicated ■ Manufacturer: Not Indicated ■ Type: Black and White ■ Postmark: Not Used
■ Value Index: B

The Lighter-Than-Airship (Blimp) has been most frequently seen with the Goodyear logo. This Blimp (the "Reliance" NC 14A) was chartered by the Canada Dry Company from Goodyear in 1940 to promote its new soft drink. On this tour for the Canada Dry Company in the Northeast part of the country, the "Reliance" was later replaced by the "Ranger" (NC 10A). Goodyear production of airships since 1917 has totalled approximately 285. The majority of these vehicles were produced for the military, with Goodyear operating approximately 25 airships for commercial purposes.

Blimps are nonrigid airships which maintain their shape from the internal pressure of the lifting gas and do not have an internal structure. Helium, the lifting gas currently used in the blimps, was initially used by Goodyear in the first of their commercial airships the "Pilgrim" in 1925. Blimps were used extensively during World War II for coastal patrol and the escorting of ship convoys. Of 89,000 ships escorted by blimps, no ship was sunk by enemy submarines.

The last of the U.S. Navy blimps were taken out of service in 1962.

This photograph is a view of the complex internal structure for the rigid type airship. Duralumin, the aluminum alloy used in the structure was developed in the U.S. by a group of Pittsburgh Metallurgists in 1921. They had spent a lengthy period of time analyzing the metal comprising the World War I German Zeppelin L-49. The Zeppelin had been downed intact. The material used in the structure of the Zeppelin had the strength of steel with only one-third the weight.

The U.S.S. "Shenandoah" (Indian name for "Daughter of the Stars") was the first U.S. built helium-filled rigid airship. Initial production of the new alloy was earmarked for construction of this air-

INTERIOR U. S. S. SHENANDOAH, NAVAL AIR STATION, LAKEHURST, N. J.   3

© CLEMENTS

Publisher: Card No. 121838, R.S. Clements, Photographer, Lakehurst, NJ ■ Manufacturer: Not Indicated ■ Type: Smooth or Pre-Linen ■ Postmark: Lakeside, CO, August 18, 192? ■ Value Index: C

ship, also designated the ZR-1 (for Zeppelin, Rigid No. 1). Construction was begun in 1922 at the Naval Aircraft Factory in the Philadelphia Navy Yard, and assembly was completed at the Lakehurst, NJ Naval Air Station. Christening of the ZR-1 occurred on October 10, 1923. The ZR-1 was powered by six Packard Engines of 650 HP each, the airship was 680 feet long with a diameter of 79 feet. After making 57 flights, the "Shenandoah" was broken in two. This loss occurred on September 3, 1925, near Ava, Ohio, there was a loss of 14 of the 43 people on board. The cause has been attributed to the violent up and down drafts of a line squall.

The airship in this photograph was manufactured by the Aircraft Development Corporation of Detroit, MI. The ZMC-2 was the only metal-skinned airship ever built. Delivered in 1929, the 150-foot long ship was also distinguished by it's unusual arrangement of eight tail fins. The one-hundredth-of-an-inch thick aluminum alloy skin eliminated helium seepage, was stronger than the fabric commonly used, and did not require constant storage in a hangar (usually only in the worst weather). The airship was flown successfully for twelve years as a training aircraft, and was dismantled in 1941. Additional funds were never appropriated to continue development of this type of airship.

U. S. NAVY METAL-CLAD AIRSHIP, NAVAL AIR STATION, LAKEHURST, N. J.

Publisher: Happy Landings Canteen, Lakehurst, NJ ■ Manufacturer: Not Indicated ■ Type: Black and White ■ Postmark: Not Used ■ Value Index: E

In this photograph, the airship is shown at Lakehurst, NJ Naval Air Station. Hangar No. 1 was completed in 1921 at a cost of $2,900,000. It has been designated a National Historic Landmark.

Publisher: Rubber City Stamp Club, Akron, OH ■ Manufacturer: Not Indicated ■ Type: Black and White
■ Postmark: Akron, OH, November 7, 1981 ■ Value Index: F

DH4B Airplane, Mitchel Field, N. Y.

Publisher: Lynbrook Post Card Company, Lynbrook, NY ■ Manufacturer: Not Indicated ■ Type: Black and White
■ Postmark: Not Used ■ Value Index: D

The U.S.S. "Macon", shown in this photograph, is in the huge Goodyear airship dock at Akron, OH, where it was built. The "Macon", or ZR-5, launched on April 21, 1933, was the last rigid airship built in the U.S. She was a sistership of the U.S.S. "Akron" (ZR-4) which was lost in a crash off the New Jersey coast 17 days earlier (April 4, 1933). The ZR-1 was the "Shenandoah", ZR-2 would have been the British-built R-38, however, it never arrived in the U.S. as it was destroyed during a test flight in England. The ZR-3 was the German-built U.S.S. "Los Angeles", which had the longest life of any rigid airship (331 flights). The airship was decommissioned in 1932 for economic reasons.

The 785-foot long U.S.S. "Macon" was the fastest airship with a speed of 87 MPH. Power was supplied by eight 12-cylinder German-built Maybach engines. The hangar space within the hull could accommodate up to five small aircraft, with four normally carried. They could be launched and retrieved in flight by hooking on to a trapeze arrangement. These Curtiss F9C-2 aircraft could thereby extend the airship's scouting range. Another feature of the "Macon" was the "Sub Cloud Car" in which an observer could be lowered through the clouds. The U.S.S. "Macon" was lost in a crash during bad weather off the coast of California on February 12, 1935. Fortunately, 81 of the 83 persons on the airship were saved. The cause of the wreck was determined to be a structural failure where a fin was attached to the hull.

The DeHaviland DH-4 series of aircraft was a British design of World War I. Many were built in the United States by Dayton-Wright Company, Standard Aircraft, and Fisher Body Company. Approximately 300 reached the battle zones prior to the Armistice. They were the only American-built plane to see combat in World War I, in addition to the flying boats used in anti-submarine operations in the English Channel and North Sea. The DH-4 was powered with the American-built Liberty Engine of 400 HP. 22,000 of these engines were built.

In 1918, 100 of the DH-4 aircraft were given to the U.S. Postal Service by the U.S. Army for airmail use. The airplane could not do the job because of design faults. Among the problems were the structure not strong enough for the heavy mail loads, the undercarriage was weak, the wheels too small, and the engines overheated. The Airmail Service undertook a modification program to correct the deficiencies for these aircraft, using four aircraft firms and the Airmail Service facility at Hazelhurst, Long Island, NY. The fuselages were covered with plywood rather than fabric for extra strength, the landing gear was reinforced and larger wheels were added. Originally, the DH-4 was designed as a two-seat reconnaissance bomber. During the modifications, the pilot's seat was moved back to the former gunner's station and the front cockpit converted for mail storage. With these changes, the DH-4 served the Airmail Service for eight years.

Many original Model DH-4s, such as the military DH-4B shown in this photograph, were also used by the barnstorming pilots at that time. Mr. James "Jimmy" Doolittle made his first of many headline appearances on September 4, 1922 when he completed the first cross-country trip in less than a day flying a Model DH-4. He flew from Florida to San Diego making one stop in 21 hours and 20 minutes.

The two-engine biplane design of the "Keystone" bomber shown in this photograph was typical of all bombers produced in the late 1920s. These aircraft followed the late World War I Martin MB design concept. Prior to the name change in 1926, the Keystone Aircraft Corporation of Bristol, PA had been the Huff-Daland Company. Their first twin-engine bombers, built in 1925, were equipped with the 400 HP Liberty engine. The use of these engines was required by the U.S. Army because of the huge war surplus that was available. The aircraft shown in the photograph was powered by the lighter and more reliable Pratt & Whitney radial engine.

Publisher: Not Indicated ■ Manufacturer: Not Indicated ■ Type: Real Photo ■ Postmark: Not Used ■ Value Index: D

These Keystone Bombers were the mainstay of the Army Air Corps for ten years. As they had not been equipped with enclosed cabins, all positions, pilot, gunner, etc., were operated from open cockpits. With a wingspan of 75 feet, these aircraft had a top speed of only 120 MPH. Early models were equipped with a twin vertical tail design.

In 1929, the Keystone Aircraft Corporation was taken over by the Curtiss-Wright Corporation, and operated as a subsidiary before being closed in 1933.

No. 361   CATAPULT PLANES OF THE CRUISERS AND BATTLESHIPS, U. S. NAVY   Official Photo U. S. Navy

Publisher: W.R. Thompson & Company, Richmond, VA ■ Manufacturer: Not Indicated ■ Type: Black and White ■ Postmark: Not Used ■ Value Index: D

Prior to the development of our large aircraft carrier fleets with their scouting squadrons, much of the scouting and patroling was done by aircraft such as these Curtiss SOC-1.

Although these aircraft continued the biplane design, the SOC-1 with its cowled engine, enclosed cockpits, and folding wings was an improvement over the Vought 03U which it replaced.

Battleships and cruisers were equipped with catapults for launching aircraft, with two or three carried on each ship. A deck-mounted crane was used to hoist the aircraft on the ship from the water.

With a crew of two (pilot and observer), the aircraft performed many other duties in addition to scouting, including the carrying of mail, rescuing downed aviators, and observing the fall of shells from their ship's big guns.

The SOC-1 was designed in 1933 and began service in 1936. Either wheel or float landing gear could be fitted to the SOCs, the latter for operations on shore when the ships were in port, for training and ferrying. The SOCs continued to be operated from some Navy combat ships through World War II.

The Grumman F3F-2 was one aircraft in a series of Navy retractable gear bi-planes. A total of 81 of Model F3F-2 aircraft were produced in 1937-38, and were used by two Marine squadrons and one Navy squadron. This model was powered with the Wright aircraft nine-cylinder "Cyclone" Engine. The previous model, F3F-1 aircraft, was fitted with the Pratt & Whitney Twin Row Engine of smaller diameter which permitted a more stream-lined nose shape. The higher power of the "Cyclone" gave the F3F-2 increased performance.

These aircraft were used from land bases or aircraft carriers and served as fighters, for scouting pur-poses, and to perfect the technique of dive-bombing. They were equipped to carry two machine guns and two 100-pound bombs. Often referred to as "Flying Barrels" because of their thick stubby shape, the top speed was 260 MPH.

The last of the F3F-2s and the F3F-3s were the end of the biplane fighters built in the U.S. The F3Fs served as the standard Navy and Marine aircraft until 1940.

An earlier aircraft of a somewhat similar design was the Curtiss BF2C-1, although it did have a retractable landing gear, it was mostly fabric-covered and did not have an enclosed cockpit.

Publisher: Not Indicated ■ Manufacturer: Not Indicated ■ Type: Real Photo ■ Postmark: Not Used ■ Value Index: C

The Douglas B-18 ("Bolo") was bomber adap-tation of the Douglas DC-2 airliner. With a wingspan of 89 feet, it was consid-ered the standard medium bomber of the late 1930s.

The armament included three machine guns and a crew of six. Its top speed was 215 MPH. A bomb load of 4,000 pounds could be carried. The B-18A had the nose section reconfig-ured with the gunner be-low the bombardier. In 1942, more than one-half of the B-18As were modi-fied to incorporate nose-mounted radar for use in antisubmarine patrol.

No. 339   LOADING BOMBS, U. S. ARMY AIR CORPS   Off. Photo U. S. Army Air Corps.

Publisher: W.R. Thompson & Company, Richmond, VA ■ Manufacturer: Not Indicated ■ Type: Black and White ■ Postmark: Savannah, GA, April 12, 1941 ■ Value Index: D

NORTH AMERICAN O-47A
U.S. ARMY AIR CORPS

The North American O-47A ("O" for Observation) was an important aircraft of the 1930s. It was designed to perform detailed observation and liaison work. The aircraft was primarily of metal construction and featured a retractable landing gear. The Wright nine-cylinder engine gave it a speed of just over 200 MPH. Its armament consisted of two 30-caliber machine guns. The crew of three included an observer positioned in the belly of the aircraft. Many National Guard units were equipped with this aircraft.

Publisher: Grogan Photo Company, Danville, IL ■ Manufacturer: Not Indicated ■ Type: Real Photo ■ Postmark: Montgomery, AL, September 3, 1943 ■ Value Index: D

As shown in this photograph, before taking their stations on a ship, catapult pilots would take their training on this land-based catapult at Jacksonville, FL Naval Air Station.

When the battleships were withdrawn from service, the role of the catapult aircraft was diminished. Also, they were being replaced by helicopters. The Vought-Sikorsky OS2U-2 aircraft in this photograph was one of the last to be used. It was important to combat action in World War II in addition to the land-based wheel model. Carrying tow depth-charges, they were used for antisubmarine patrol and directing the ship gunfire.

Another single float monoplane somewhat similar to this OS2U-2, with an inline engine, was the Curtiss SO3C "Seagull".

OS2U-2 BEING CATAPULTED
N.A.S. JACKSONVILLE, FLORIDA

Publisher: Not Indicated ■ Manufacturer: Not Indicated ■ Type: Real Photo ■ Postmark: Not Used ■ Value Index: D

Catapults used during World War II were operated by a combination of compressed air and hydraulic fluid.

Modern catapults that do not require the aircraft to be mounted on a carriage are used on the new aircraft carriers. These new catapults reduce the space required for take-offs, thereby permitting more aircraft to be landed and stored on the ship.

Publisher: Lou Kramer, Grayling, MI ■ Manufacturer: Not Indicated ■ Type: Real Photo
■ Postmark: Not Used ■ Value Index: D

The Seversky P-35, shown in this photograph, was a product of the company founded by Russian exile Alexander P. DeSeversky who would later become well-known for his best-selling book VICTORY THROUGH AIR POWER (published in 1942).

The P-35 was the first of the new breed of monoplane fighters in service with the all-metal construction, retractable landing gear, and enclosed cockpit.

An order for 76 of this model was delivered to the U.S. Army Air Corps beginning in July of 1937. The following year, the Curtiss P-36, a fighter of similar characteristics, became available.

Several of the P-35 were obtained by wealthy sportsmen pilots and flown in the National Air Races. The aircraft won the Bendix Trophy Race in 1937, 1938, and 1939.

A two-seat version of the P-35 was built by Seversky for export to Japan, and later both single seater and two-place versions for Sweden. At the outbreak of World War II, one-half of the Swedish single-place order had been delivered, plus two of the two-place model. The U.S. Army took over the remaining 60 aircraft, and a portion of the single-place EP-1 aircraft were used as P-35s in combat against the Japanese in the Philippines, while the two-place 2PAs were used as AT-12 advance trainers.

In 1939, the Seversky Company became the Republic Aircraft Corporation, producer of the Model P-47 "Thunderbolt" Fighter of World War II fame.

Although the Air Corps and U.S. Navy had both given up biplane fighters, the biwing design prevailed for the trainers that most Army and Navy cadets used during World War II.

The aircraft shown in this photograph were popularly known as the "Stearman", and they were occasionally referred to as "Boeing" when the Stearman Company became a division of Boeing in 1939.

The model designations were PT-13 series for the Army and N2S-2, 3, or 5 for the Navy when powered with the 220 HP Lycoming engine or PT-17 series for the Army and N2S-1 or 4 for the Navy when using the Continental engine of 220 HP.

BOEING PT-17'S, HAWTHORNE SCHOOL OF AERONAUTICS ORANGEBURG, S. C.

27867

Publisher: Not Indicated ■ Manufacturer: Asheville Post Card Company, Asheville, NC ■ Type: Black and White ■ Postmark: Not Used ■ Value Index: D

Following World War II, the Stearman trainer could be purchased as war surplus at a low cost, and many were used for crop dusting. Among the approximately 2,000 of these aircraft that are currently registered, many have larger engines of 450 and even 600 HP for use in aerobatic demonstrations.

NR-1 FORMATION (9 RYAN PRIMARY TRAINERS)

Publisher: Not Indicated ■ Manufacturer: Not Indicated ■ Type: Real Photo ■ Postmark: Great Lakes, IL, November 21, 1942 ■ Value Index: D

One of the primary trainer aircraft used by U.S. Naval Aviation Cadets was the Ryan NR-1. A low-wing monoplane with metal fusilage, it was the Navy version of the Air Corps PT-21 aircraft.

This military trainer was derived from the civilian Model ST (Sport Trainer) powered with the inline Menasco engine. The appealing streamlining of the Menasco-powered aircraft made it one of the most popular designs of all time. It was chosen for use in many highly popular pictures such as, "Too Hot To Handle", "Test Pilot", and "Dive Bomber".

For the military trainers, the Menasco engine was replaced with the more reliable radial Kinner engine. Other changes included the addition of a sweepback of slightly more than four degrees to the wings to cause the aircraft to stall and spin more easily. Prior to this change, the aircraft was considered too docile for the students who would be going on to fly the more agile fighter planes.

Small numbers of an export version (STM) with 150 HP Menasco engines were shipped to Mexico, Honduras, and Guatamala. Another 108 of STMs of this model were operated in Java and by the Royal Dutch Army and Navy.

The most widely-used aircraft for the second phase or basic training for Air Force Cadets was the Consolidated-Vultee, Model BT-13 "Valiant" or "Vibrator" as it was referred to by some cadets who thought its flying characteristics were not the smoothest.

The aircraft are shown in this photograph in echelon formation. Approximately 8,700 of this model were produced. Some aircraft were BT-15s with Wright instead of Pratt & Whitney engines. In Navy service, the designations were SNV-1 and SNV-2.

A much heavier aircraft than the primary trainers, it had a larger engine of 450 HP. A sliding cockpit enclosure was also provided. In addition, the students flying this trainer would experience their first use of two-way radio communication, the use of landing flaps, and the control of a variable pitch propeller.

Publisher: Southern Bell Telephone and Telegraph Company, Inc. ■ Manufacturer: Not Indicated ■ Type: Black and White ■ Postmark: Macon, GA, June 12, 1944 ■ Value Index: D

The third or advanced phase of Air Force Cadet training was accomplished in this North American Aviation Corporation trainer designated AT-6 (Texan) for the Air Corps and SNJ for the Navy.

This all-metal aircraft was similar to the basic trainer; however, it featured a retractable landing gear and a larger engine of 600 HP.

With a top speed of 212 MPH, its performance characteristics served to prepare the cadet for his transition to fighter aircraft. With the ability to climb to 24,000 feet, the AT-6 provided the student with training in the use of oxygen.

Over 10,000 of this model were produced in the U.S. and Canada.

Publisher: Not Indicated ■ Manufacturer: Grogan Photo Company, Danville, IL ■ Type: Real Photo ■ Postmark: Not Used ■ Value Index: D

Those in Royal Air Force and Royal Canadian Airforce use were known as "Harvards".

The "Texan" also saw service in the Korean War for marking targets to be attacked by the fighter-bombers.

A large number are in private operations today in various capacities, some being used for aerobatic demonstrations and a group of eleven of the "Texans" are operated by the Sky-Typers for aerial advertising.

21—Advanced Training Plane, Air Corps Advanced Flying School, Turner Field, Albany, Ga.

PHOTOGRAPH BY U. S. ARMY AIR CORPS

Publisher: Georgia Cigar & Tobacco Company, Albany, GA ■ Manufacturer: Curteich, Chicago, IL ■ Type: Linen
■ Postmark: Albany, GA, May 22, 1942 ■ Value Index: D

Those aviation cadets designated to fly other than the single-engine fighter aircraft would be required to take additional training in a twin-engine trainer such as this Curtiss AT-9 to acquire multi-engine experience.

The AT-9 "Fledgling" or "Jeep" as it was more commonly called entered training service in 1942. The original prototype was a fabric-covered machine. All production AT-9s were metal covered.

The AT-9 was not a particularly easy airplane to fly, it did acquaint students with the characteristics they would be encountering in the high performance twin-engine bombers and fighters. A total of 791 of all models of the AT-9 were produced.

One of the last known survivors of this model trainer was recently restored and put on display in the new modern flight gallery of the Air Force Museum at Wright-Patterson Air Force Base, Dayton, OH.

U.S. Air Corps crew training, where the pilot, copilot, bombardier, and navigator learned to work as a team was intended to be completed in the type of aircraft shown in this photograph. Only one of the Ranger powered AT-14 was built, and prior to it one Pratt & Whitney powered AT-13 was built. This latter aircraft was later designated the AT-21 when the Army changed its requirements to that of a gunnery trainer.

Construction of the AT-14, later the AT-21, was 85 percent wood. The Duramold process was employed using plasticized laminated plywood.

Production of the airplane was slow in starting. The Fairchild Company was having labor union

FAIRCHILD AT-14 BOMBER CREW TRAINER
(2 RANGER 12 ENGINES)

Publisher: Not Indicated ■ Manufacturer: Grogan Photo, Danville, IL ■ Type: Real Photo
■ Postmark: Nashville, TN, October 5, 1943 ■ Value Index: D

problems, the Army was continually insisting on engineering changes, and the Duramold process did not seem to be suitable for mass production techniques. Although 175 aircraft were built, only a few were sent into actual service as crews received their training in early production bombers or in bombers that were returned from the war fronts for that purpose.

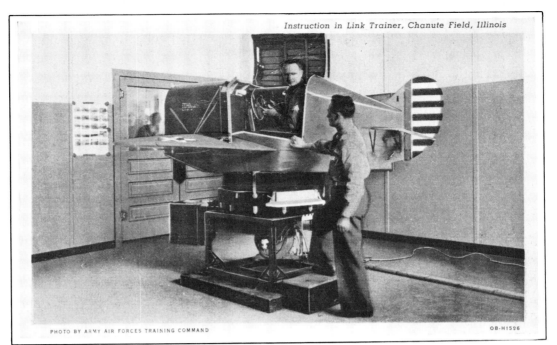

Instruction in Link Trainer, Chanute Field, Illinois

PHOTO BY ARMY AIR FORCES TRAINING COMMAND

OB-H1596

In addition to their actual flying training, aviation cadets also spent time in a Link Trainer. Safer and cheaper than using real aircraft, the trainer was able to simulate blind flying conditions, thereby, permitting the student to practice instrument flying techniques at any time without leaving the ground.

Publisher: Not Indicated ■ Manufacturer: Curteich, Chicago, IL ■ Type: Linen ■ Postmark: Not Used ■ Value Index: E

Mr. Edwin A. Link worked as a teen-ager in his father's player piano and organ factory in Binghamton, NY. He combined his interest in aviation with his knowledge of player piano mechanisms to develop the trainer, which is essentially a pneumatically-operated device. Over 3,000 of these were built in the World War II era; they formed the basis of an industry which today produces highly sophisticated flight simulators that are able to duplicate almost any flight conditions.

AIRPLANE MECHANICS WORKING ON A TRAINER AT KEESLER FIELD---BILOXI, MISS
PHOTO BY ARMY AIR FORCES TECHNICAL TRAINING COMMAND
KEEP 'EM FLYING

Publisher: Not Indicated ■ Manufacturer: Gulfport Printing Company, Gulfport, MS ■ Type: Smooth-White Border ■ Postmark: Not Used ■ Value Index: E

U.S. Air Corps Mechanics are shown receiving "on the job training" as they perform maintenance on this basic trainer.

To save time, mechanics were usually trained to be specialists in one particular area, including hydraulics, propellers, sheet metal, engines, etc. At air field operations, a Crew Chief is assigned to oversee the total maintenance on each airplane.

The mechanics were often the unsung heros in some of the combat zones where they were able to keep aircraft aloft with less than the required equipment and facilities. In some areas, this work was accomplished during enemy attack.

P-40, Selfridge Field, Mich

Publisher: Not Indicated ■ Manufacturer: Not Indicated ■ Type: Real Photo
■ Postmark: Selfridge Field, MI, February 4, 1943 ■ Value Index: D

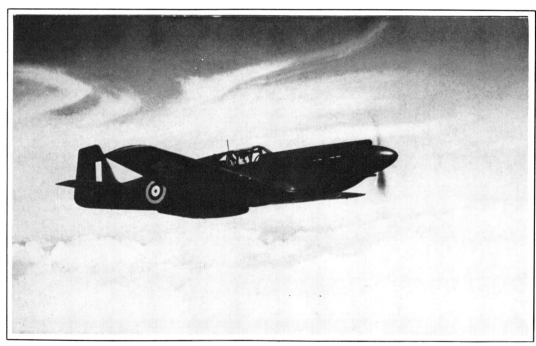

Publisher: Not Indicated ■ Manufacturer: Wesco Color Card ■ Type: Chrome ■ Postmark: Not Used
■ Value Index: D

The Curtiss P-40 is probably best remembered for the operations with General Claire Chennault and his Flying Tigers. The aircraft were painted with a shark-mouth motif on the nose. The aircraft was available in larger quantities than any other fighter at the outbreak of World War II. Unfortunately, the P-40 was not a match for the much lighter and more maneuverable Japanese "Zero".

In the attack on Pearl Harbor in December 1941, 55 P-40s were destroyed on the ground. Approximately 13,700 of the aircraft were produced by the end of 1944. Many of these aircraft were located in Africa, Italy, and with the British and French Air Forces. They were also stationed in the Aleutian Islands for defense purposes.

As were most military aircraft, the P-40 came in many configurations as the combat conditions dictated the required modifications. The original P-40 was powered with an Allison Engine and had one 0.30 cal. and one 0.50 cal. machine gun firing through the propeller arc. The P-40D in addition to some minor changes had four machine guns mounted in the wings. The Model P-40E was equipped with six wing-mounted guns. The P-40F had the Rolls-Royce Merlin Engine as a replacement for the Allison Engine. Also, during later production the fuselage was lengthened 19 inches to enhance lateral stability.

The 5000 P-40N aircraft had a redesigned canopy and used Allison Engines as the Merlin Engine production was required for the P-51 fighters. Production of Merlin and Allison powered models was intermingled on the production line in the F, K, L, and M series.

The initial flights, in October of 1940, of the North American P-51 "Mustang" (initially called the "Apache") were the result of a large effort. The aircraft had been designed and built to British specifications in only 117 days. The early "Mustangs", as shown in the photograph, were operated by the British RAF.

The P-51B and P-51C had the original Allison Engines replaced with the Packard-built Merlin Engine to improve the aircraft performance at higher altitudes.

As a result of approximately 8,000 being built, the Model P-51D became the most widely known version of this aircraft. It had a redesigned bubble canopy and six 0.50 cal. machine guns. Its speed was 437 MPH. The last and slightly faster of the series was the P-51H, approximately 500 were delivered prior to Victory-Japan Day.

Though performing many duties such as interceptor, dive bomber, etc., a major role of the U.S. Army Air Force P-51 was the escorting of bombers, both the B-17s in Europe and the B-29s to Japan from Iwo Jima.

Some of America's top aces flying the "Mustang" were Major George Preddy with 26 victories, Lt. Colonel John C. Meyer with 24 victories, Captain Don Gentile with 21 victories and Captain Charles Yaeger with 11 victories. The Model P-51 "Mustang" was used extensively in the Korean conflict and was the last Air Force propellor— driven fighter in operation.

There are many privately-owned "Mustangs" today with some taking part in the unlimited class of the National Air Races.

The Model P-47 "Thunderbolt", built by the Republic Aircraft Corporation (formerly Seversky Aircraft) was the heaviest of all single-engine operational fighter aircraft. Its weight was due not only to its size, but to an abundance of armor which allowed it to be a successful ground attack airplane.

Of 15,675 "Thunderbolts" produced, 12,600 were the P-47D. The bubble shown in this photograph replaced the original cockpit design which blended into the tail (commonly called the razorback design) in part of the "D" model. The top speed of the Model P-47D was 429 MPH, however an experimental cleaned-up lightweight model, the XP-47J was the first piston-engine fighter to exceed 500 MPH (504 MPH in level flight).

Publisher: Not Indicated ■ Manufacturer: Ian Allen (Printing) Ltd. ■ Type: Chrome ■ Postmark: Not Used ■ Value Index: E

The ruggedness of the "Thunderbolt" led to its nickname "Jug" (for juggernaut). Another tribute to its toughness was the fact that all ten of the top "Thunderbolt" aces had survived the war. Two notable P-47 aces were Lt.Colonel Francis Gabreski with 28 victories and Colonel Hubert Zemke with 17.

P-38 "Lightenings" Starting to Peel Off, March Field, California

The aircraft shown in this photograph was designed to be a high altitude interceptor. The Lockheed P-38 "Lightening" did not prove to be a good aircraft when initially deployed in the European Theatre of Operations. The extreme cold at high altitudes caused malfunctioning of its superchargers, engines, and the cockpit heating system. Its unusual shape may have also contributed to loses higher than any other fighter aircraft. It could not be mistaken as a friendly aircraft by the enemy as was often the case with the P-51 and the P-47 which resembled the German ME-109 and FW-190 respectively. Improvements were made in later models of the P-38 but it was generally re-

Publisher: Western Publishing & Novelty Company, Los Angeles, CA ■ Manufacturer: C.T. Art-Colortone ■ Type: Linen ■ Postmark: March Field, CA, March 8, 1946 ■ Value Index: D

placed for use over Europe by the P-51 and P-47. The P-38 performed more successfully in the warmer Pacific Ocean operations.

Probably the most significant action by P-38s occurred on April 18, 1943 when a flight of 16 aircraft intercepted and destroyed the Japanese Mitsubishi Bomber carrying Japanese Admiral Yamamoto over Bougainville. The P-38s accomplished this victory after a flight of 435 miles from Guadalcanal.

Captain Richard Bong, the leading U.S. Ace acquired all of his 40 victories while flying the P-38. McGuire Air Force Base in New Jersey is named in honor of Captain Bong's nearest rival, Major Thomas B. McGuire who had 38 victories in the same type of aircraft.

Publisher: Not Indicated ■ Manufacturer: Uitgave, "Rembrandt", Amsterdam ■ Type: Black and White
■ Postmark: Not Used ■ Value Index: D

The Brewster F2A Navy Fighter has been the subject of much controversy, It made a poor showing at the Battle of Midway on June 4, 1942. By then it had already been relegated to a fighter-trainer status and being exported to several foreign countries.

The F2A was nearly a ton heavier and 30 MPH slower than the Japanese Zero Fighter. The armament was also lighter with four machine guns compared to the Japanese Zero with two 20 mm cannons and two machine guns.

In defense of the Model F2A it should be noted that the Battle of Midway was the first combat mission for the squadron using the aircraft. The pilots had very little familiarization with the technical advances of this first monoplane fighter. The new features included hydraulic wing flaps and retractable landing gear, controllable pitch propellers, engine with supercharger and an oxygen system. The F4F Wildcats also being used there, in similar circumstances, performed much better.

Several cases of landing gear failure due to the stress of arrested carrier landings caused the F2A to be withdrawn from aircraft carrier operations. There were instances of sabotage to the arresting hook on several of the F2As, probably occurring at the factory.

Of the Navy's order for 163 aircraft, 44 were diverted to Finland for combating the Russians. The Finns had the most success with the F2A because their early model was much lighter than those that followed. Also, the Curtiss-Wright engine which had suffered from overheating in the Pacific area, was not likely to do so in the cold climate of Finland.

Most of the 170 "Buffalo" ordered by the British were sent to defend Singapore and Burma as they did not seem able to compete with the German fighters. These aircraft, and those acquired by the Dutch, as shown in the photograph also performed poorly against the Japanese fighters. The nickname "Buffalo" was bestowed by the British.

Publisher: Not Indicated ▪ Manufacturer: Not Indicated ▪ Type: Black and White ▪ Postmark: Not Used
▪ Value Index: D

Publisher: Goodyear Aircraft Company ▪ Manufacturer: Not Indicated ▪ Type: Chrome
▪ Postmark: Not Used ▪ Value Index: D

By 1942, the Grumman F4F "Wildcat" had become the standard Navy Shipboard Fighter aircraft. The Brewster F2A had been the first of the monoplane type, but was not acceptable in combat operations.

While the new "Wildcat" fighters had more guns (six machine guns) and had better protective armor than the Japanese Zero, they were still slightly slower and less maneuverable. To overcome these deficiencies the pilots had adapted new and different combat tactics and the final totals showed seven enemy aircraft destroyed for each "Wildcat" lost.

Over 5,000 of the "Wildcat" design were produced by the Eastern Aircraft Division of the General Motors Corporation and identified as the FM-1 which was identical to the F4F-4 except for having four machine guns rather than six. The FM-2 which had a taller fin and rudder used a Curtiss-Wright Engine instead of the Pratt & Whitney Engine on the Model FM-1.

"Wildcats" played a large part in the Battle of Guadalcanal and many were in operation aboard the smaller escort aircraft carriers later in the War. Some outstanding "Wildcat" pilots were Marine ace Joe Foss, later to become Governor of South Dakota with 26 victories and Lt. J.E. Swett who downed seven Japanese bombers within a 15-minute period.

The Chance-Vought F4U "Corsair" was the first American fighter plane with speed in excess of 400 MPH (Maximum speed was approximately 420 MPH). The "Corsair" was also referred to as the "Bent-Wing Bird" due to its inverted gull-wing design. This design was necessary to provide clearance for the large three-blade propeller that was required. The first combat mission for the F4U occurred over the Solomon Islands on February 13, 1943. Many Marine squadrons were equipped with the "Corsair" including the "Black Sheep" Squadron of the well— known "Pappy" Boyington, an ace with 20 victories.

Beside being an excellent fighter aircraft the F4U proved to be an excellent dive bomber and ground-attack aircraft. The "Corsair" was not approved for aircraft carrier duty until August of 1944, due mainly to poor landing characteristics and poor forward vision for the pilot in the landing atitude from the rear-mounted cockpit. Both problems were largely overcome by the installation of a longer tail wheel strut.

To be accommodated on British aircraft carriers, "Corsairs" used by the British had eight inches removed from each wingtip. This change caused the aircraft to have a slightly higher stalling speed.

A night-fighter model of the "Corsair" featured a radar antenna pod mounted on the right wing. In late 1944, a much improved model, the F4U-4 was introduced. This aircraft could be distinguished by the additional air-scoop at the bottom of the engine cowling and the four-blade propeller required by the more powerful engine.

By the end of the Pacific Theatre operations the records showed eleven enemy aircraft destroyed by "Corsairs" for each loss of a "Corsair". Approximately one-half of the fighter-bomber combat missions flown in the Korean War were by "Corsairs".

Production of these aircraft did not cease until 1952 after a ten-year period. The records indicate 4,014 "Corsairs" were also produced by Goodyear Aircraft as the FG-1 and 735 manufactured by Brewster Aeronautical Corporation were the F3A-1. Goodyear F2G "Corsairs" with 3000 HP Pratt & Whitney Engines, were modified by civilian owners for air racing and won the Thompson Trophy Race in 1947 and 1949.

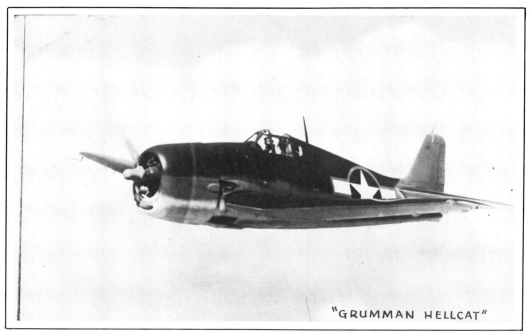

"GRUMMAN HELLCAT"

Publisher: Not Indicated ■ Manufacturer: Not Indicated ■ Type: Real Photo ■ Postmark: Not Used
■ Value Index: D

FLYING FORTRESS B-17 IN FLIGHT—042

Publisher: Not Indicated ■ Manufacturer: E.C. Kropp Company, Milwaukee, WI ■ Type: Linen
■ Postmark: Pittsburgh, PA, May 29, 1958 ■ Value Index: F

The Grumman F6F "Hellcat", shown in this photograph, was designed early in 1941 and modified after the attack at Pearl Harbor. The design was influenced by the results of flight tests on a Japanese Zero that had been forced down in the Aleutian Islands.

The wingspan of the "Hellcat" was only five feet greater than its predecessor, the F4F "Wildcat" but it weighed about two tons more. However, with the large Pratt & Whitney R-2800-10, 18-cylinder, Twin-Row Engine it had the speed and climbing ability to out-maneuver the Japanese Zero. Water injection was added in 1944. The top speed of the F6F was 390 MPH (about 60 MPH faster than the F4F "Wildcat"). It's armament consisted of six 0.50 caliber machine guns mounted in the wings.

Of all the enemy aircraft shot down by carrier-based aircraft in World War II, the "Hellcat" accounted for 75 percent. A total of 12,272 "Hellcats" were built and approximately 1,200 went to the British. The Navy operated many F6Fs for several years after World War II.

The evolution of the "Flying Fortress" began in 1935 with an order for one B-17 (Model 299), then in 1936 for 13 Model 299B or B-17B aircraft, and in 1938 with an order for 39 of the B-17B. The other models progressed as follows: the B-17C in 1939 with 38 built; the B-17D in 1941 with 42 built; the B-17E in 1941 with 512 built; the B-17F in 1942 with 3,405 built; and, the B-17G in 1943 with 8,680 built.

Other than the installation of progressively improved engines and internal modifications such as new electrical systems and fuel tanks, visible changes included, the B-17C had a longer ventral blister and the removal of the two side blisters. The B-17D had engine cowl flaps. The B-17E had the top and tail turrets added and the larger vertical tail with an extended vertical fin along the top of the fuselage. The B-17F had the landing gear strengthened to support the 20,800-pound bomb load. The B-17G had the addition of a chin turret with twin machine guns. Prior to the installation of this chin turret on the late model B-17Fs, the B-17 was vulnerable to frontal attacks by enemy fighter aircraft.

Large numbers of the B-17 were used in the European Theatre and while the aircraft could withstand extensive damage, there were heavy losses because they did not have good fighter escorts.

Two B-17G aircraft were used by the Pratt & Whitney and Wright Companies for testing turboprop engines. The engines were mounted in the nose of the aircraft. Several of the aircraft were converted for borate and water bombing of forest fires. Approximately ten of these aircraft are flying today with many on static display in museums.

LIBERATOR (B-24) Bomber. Assailing the enemy on many war fronts it ranges over 3000 miles. Has a maximum speed of over 300 m.p.h. CONSOLIDATED VULTEE AIRCRAFT CORP. San Diego Div. San Diego, Cal.

Publisher: Not Indicated ■ Manufacturer: Not Indicated ■ Type: Real Photo ■ Postmark: Not Used ■ Value Index: D

Pupils' Bonds Buy Bombers

Publisher: Theodore Roosevelt Junior High School, Germantown, PA ■ Manufacturer: Not Indicated ■ Type: Black and White ■ Postmark: Not Used ■ Value Index: D

The Consolidated B-24 "Liberator", though not as well known as the B-17 was in some respects a superior bomber. Designed in 1939, five years after the B-17, it incorporated the technical improvements that had been gained during five years of B-17 production.

The tricycle landing gear provided easier and safer take-offs and landings, and its long narrow wing provided excellent performance. One flaw was the high-lift airfoils causing some instability at very high altitudes and at low speeds. The B-24 was also equipped with an autopilot that helped it complete long-range missions such as the one from North Africa to the Ploesti, Roumania Oil Refineries. Two hundred B-24s were converted to C-109 tanker aircraft for hauling fuel to the B-29s in China that would be bombing Japan. Transport versions of the B-24 were designated as the C-87 aircraft.

In Naval service, the "Liberator" was identified as the PB4Y-1. Later the PB4Y-2, "Privateer", distinguished externally by its single tail fin, was developed. Other differences included two top gun turrets, two side gun blisters, and seven feet added to the length of the fuselage. Over 18,000 "Liberators" were produced, more than any other U.S. aircraft for the war effort. In addition to Consolidated, they were built by North American Aviation, Douglas Aircraft, and Ford Motor Company at their Willow Run, MI factory. Several were converted for executive use by corporations including the Continental Can Company.

The story of the disappearance of the B-24 "Lady Be Good" in 1943 and its discovery sixteen years later has been recorded in a book by that name.

Nicknamed the "Mitchell" for General William "Billy" Mitchell, the controversial advocate of a separate Air Force, the North American B-25 was one of the Air Corp's three main medium bombers used in World War II, the other two were the Martin B-26 "Marauder" and the Douglas A-20 "Havoc".

As with most military aircraft, the B-25 came in many models, from the original B-25 through the B-25J. The principle differences among the models was the upgrading of engines and the rearrangement of armament to suit changing combat conditions. As examples, the B-25G and H initially had a 75mm gun in the nose while later model B-25Js carried up to twelve forward-firing machine guns.

The B-25 came into prominence when it was used to bomb Tokyo. Sixteen of the bombers led by Lt. Colonel James Doolittle flew this mission flying from the Aircraft Carrier "Hornet" on April 18, 1942.

During World War II, a common practice was for organizations to designate the funds they collected or from their war bond purchases to acquire a particular item. In this example, the B-25 shown in this photograph was purchased with the $175,000 from war bond sales by the pupils of Theodore Roosevelt Junior High School of Germantown, PA. The aircraft was named "Rough Rider" by them for "Teddy" Roosevelt.

In the post war years, many B-25s were in civilian use as executive transports, water bombers for fighting forest fires, and as camera platforms for the making of motion pictures such as the "Battle of Britain".

Publisher: Not Indicated ■ Manufacturer: Not Indicated ■ Type: Real Photo ■ Postmark: Not Used
■ Value Index: D

The Boeing B-29 "Superfortress" with a wingspan of 141 feet and a gross weight of 124,000 pounds was the largest bomber of World War II. It was also a more complex aircraft, as the first military aircraft with pressurized sections for the crew members. The separate forward and rear bomb bays required a special mechanism to permit the alternate release of bombs from the two areas in order to maintain the proper balance in the aircraft. The engines were 2000 HP Wright R-3350s.

The heavy defensive armament consisting of a 20mm cannon and 12 machine guns in remotely controlled turrets allowed formations of up to 500 B-29 aircraft to strike at Japan with practically no fighter escorts.

The atomic bombing of Hiroshima, Japan on August 6, 1945 was accomplished by the B-29 "Enola Gay" and on August 9, 1945 the B-29 "Bockscar" brought the same fate to Nagasaki, Japan.

The B-29 also was in action during all but a few days of the lengthy Korean War, with losses of only 20 aircraft due to enemy action. For aerial refueling purposes, the KB-29M Tanker Aircraft was developed, using a trailing hose system and the KB-29P Tanker Aircraft with the single tail boom system.

A much improved aircraft made of higher strength aluminum and with Pratt & Whitney 3000 HP 28 Cylinder Engines was originally to have been the B-29D. The new aircraft was finally designated as the B-50 and was easily recognized by its five-foot taller vertical fin.

No. 501 The VECA "Ventura", U. S. Navy Torpedo Bomber   Official U. S. Navy Photo.

Publisher: Not Indicated ■ Manufacturer: Not Indicated ■ Type: Black and White ■ Postmark: Not Used
■ Value Index: D

The PV-1 "Ventura" was built by the Vega Aircraft Corporation, a subsidiary of the Lockheed Company. It was developed from the civilian Lockheed Model 18 "Lodestar".

The aircraft was too large for aircraft carrier use. It was operated from land bases for reconnaissance and antisubmarine patrol.

A torpedo, as shown in this photograph, or conventional bomb loads could be carried internally. The PV-1 was a considerable improvement over the Lockheed "Hudson" Bomber as it included a lower rear gun position not included on the "Hudson". Most variants of the "Ventura" included the top gun turret as on the "Hudson".

Many Lockheed "Hudsons" were operated by the British and French Air Forces and by the U.S. Air Forces as the B-14.

The Consolidated PBY "Catalina" was built in larger numbers than any other flying boat, over 3,000, beginning in 1935. The narrow pylon supporting the 104-foot wing served to house the flight engineer's station. It was the first seaplane to be equipped with wing floats that retracted to form the tip of the wing.

A civilian PBY was the first flying boat to make a Transcontinental flight on June 24, 1937, and on July 6, 1939 this same aircraft completed the first round-the-world flight by seaplane.

The last few PBY-4s were the first aircraft of this series to have blister-type side mounted gun turrets. The PBY-5A was the first of the amphibious types with a tricycle landing gear for land operation.

PBY-4 PATROL BOMBER
Official U. S. Navy Photo

Publisher: The Mayrose Co., Publishers, NY ■ Manufacturer: Not Indicated ■ Type: Black and White
■ Postmark: Not Used ■ Value Index: E

The rugged and long-ranging PBY served many duties in World War II, including patrol, torpedo plane and bomber, convoy escort, and was responsible for the rescue of many downed airmen..

A PBY was credited with locating the German Battleship "Bismark" and maintaining surveillance until the British Battle Force arrived to sink the ship. A patrolling "Catalina" also discovered the big Japanese Fleet heading for Midway Island. This early warning played a part in the American victory in the Battle of Midway.

Publisher: The Mayrose Co., Publishers, NY ■ Manufacturer: Not Indicated ■ Type: Black and White
■ Postmark: Not Used ■ Value Index: E

Publisher: Not Indicated ■ Manufacturer: Not Indicated ■ Type: Linen
■ Postmark: New York, NY, July 31, 1942 ■ Value Index: F

The TBF "Avenger" was a Grumman design; however, 7,546 of the total 9,839 that were produced were manufactured by the Eastern Aircraft Division of General Motors Corporation, and designated the TBM. It was designed as a replacement for the aging Douglas TBD "Devestator". The TBD had only been with the fleet for a few years when the TBF was designed.

The "Avenger" carried a three-man crew and the majority were armed with two machine guns in the wing and one each in the dorsal turret and the ventral position. This aircraft was the first production (Great Lakes XTBG-1 had an internal carriage 1935-1936) torpedo plane to carry its torpedo or bombs internally, which increased the speed over an externally mounted load. One of the aircraft's few weaknesses was a poor rate of climb because of a gross weight of almost eight tons.

Five of the six "Avengers" taking part in the Battle of Midway were shot down. This loss was attributed to poor battle tactics rather than the fault of the aircraft, and it soon became the standard carrier-based torpedo bomber.

The "Avenger" was used in large numbers by the British Royal Navy during World War II and in the middle 1950s when additional TBM-3Es were supplied under Mutual Defense Assistance Plans due to delays in the development and production of the "Fairly Gannet" for British Royal Navy Carrier Antisubmarine Service.

After World War II, TBMs were used extensively in the post-war Navy. Many of the aircraft were modified for Airborne Early Warning operations and antisubmarine warfare. A few surplus "Avengers" were modified for combating forest fires by dropping water and chemicals.

Design of the Curtiss SB2C "Helldiver" began in 1938. It did not reach operational status until Fall 1943. It was intended to replace the Curtiss SBC biplane and the nearly obsolete Douglas SBD "Dauntless". The production of the SB2C was slow and some of the "Dauntless" dive bombers were retained until the end of World War II.

The aircraft was slow to develop as a result of 900 engineering changes made in attempts to overcome some of the design problems that included cooling and directional stability.

Some of the changes were restricted by the fact that the overall dimensions had to be maintained at a size that would permit two of the aircraft to fit on the standard 40 foot by 48 foot carrier deck elevator.

The Model XSB2C-1 shown in this photograph would have been equipped with four machine guns in the wing. With the four guns later replaced by two 20mm cannon, the aircraft became the Model SB2C-1C.

A total of 900 aircraft ordered by the Army Air Corps were identified as the A-25. Nearly one-half of these aircraft were delivered to the U.S. Navy for use by the Marines. The Brewster SB2A "Buccaneer" was very similar in appearance to the Curtiss SB2C, although 771 were produced only a few were placed in service for training purposes. As America's last dive bomber of World War II, the Curtiss SB2C "Helldiver" set an impressive record at the later Pacific battles of Leyte Gulf, the Philippine Sea, and Rabaul.

At the end of World War II, a large number of surplus aircraft became available for civilian purposes.

Stearman, formerly primary trainers, could be had for a few hundred dollars and proved to be very practical aircraft for the aerial application of pesticides in the farming areas.

The biplane-type aircraft were preferred for this type of work because of

Publisher: Card No. C14276, Not Indicated ■ Manufacturer: Not Indicated ■ Type: Chrome ■ Postmark: Not Used ■ Value Index: F

their better maneuverability. Also, at that time there were no aircraft being built specifically for this purpose.

The aircraft shown in this photograph had the wing tips modified to improve their performance. These Stearman trainers of the LiCalzi Air Service were also modified by replacing the front cockpit with a hopper capable of holding approximately 1000 pounds of pesticides.

Publisher: Card No. 58211, Kunkel Aerial Surveys, Summerfield, FL ■ Manufacturer: Not Indicated ■ Type: Chrome ■ Postmark: Not Used ■ Value Index: F

This photograph shows a Stearman aircraft sprayer of S.W. Hanke of Clio, SC using a liquid pesticide to treat a tomato field. These aircraft may also be rigged to dispense a dry-type chemical. This Stearman and many others were modified with new engines using the Pratt & Whitney Wasp Junior Engine. This engine provided twice the power of the original engine used in the Stearman.

Two of the first aircraft produced specifically for spraying and dusting were Piper Aircraft's "Pawnee" of 1959 and Cessna's "Ag-Wagon" in 1966. These two monoplanes were of similar design, with ease of handling being a characteristic of each, together with cockpits that offered ample vision and maximum protection for the pilots.

The Cessna "Ag-Wagon" included a hopper of 200 gallon capacity. This aircraft never achieved the popularity of the Piper "Pawnee". A popular biplane also designed for this purpose is the Grumman "Ag-Cat".

As previously indicated, another important use for surplus military aircraft is a water bomber to fight forest fires.

This photograph shows one of the two Martin "Mars" flying boats operated by Fire Industries Flying Tankers on Vancouver Island, British Columbia. These flying boats can pick up approximately 7,000 gallons of water in 20 seconds from the surface of a lake, and have proven to be very effective against forest fires.

The Martin "Mars" with a wingspan of 200 feet had the largest wingspan of any flying boat to be used in military service. The prototype aircraft with twin vertical fins was designated Model XPB2M-1 and intended to be a pa-

Publisher: Card No. 653, 105237, Stelling Agencies Ltd., Box 465, Sta. A, Vancouver 1, B.C., Canada
■ Manufacturer: Not Indicated ■ Type: Chrome ■ Postmark: Not Used ■ Value Index: D

trol bomber. It was later converted for transport use and called the Model XPB2M-1R. A short production run delivered only six aircraft for transport service. All of these aircraft had single vertical fins. Five of these flying boats were JRM-1s equipped with the Curtiss-Wright Engines of 2300 HP. The last aircraft, the JRM-2, used four Pratt & Whitney Engines of 3000 HP each.

During the years immediately after World War II, many corporations converted some of the surplus military aircraft for executive use. The Douglas DC-3 (exmilitary C-47) and the DC-4 (exmilitary C-54) were most popular for this purpose. Many medium bombers such as the Model B-25 and the A-26 were also utilized. The aircraft shown in this photograph was an example of a special sales operation rather than an executive usage. The Atlas Tire Company obtained very useful advertising with this Douglas Model DC-4 as a flying showroom and dealer meeting room.

In recent years, many corporations have been reluctant to display their logo on the aircraft they

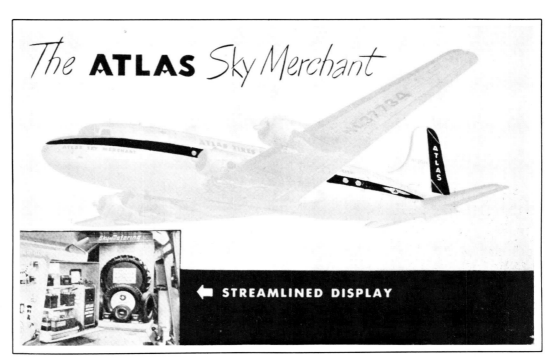

Publisher: Not Indicated ■ Manufacturer: Not Indicated ■ Type: Chrome ■ Postmark: Not Used
■ Value Index: B

use because of criticism from several sources (unions, stockholders, customers, etc.) regarding the expense of operating their aviation departments.

The fate of many former military aircraft was to become a gate-guard or memorial.

This Lockheed P-38 was developed into a memorial for Major Richard I. Bong and is located at his home town of Poplar, Wisconsin. Major Bong flew this type of fighter aircraft against the Japanese to become America's highest scoring ace with forty victories.

On the day that Hiroshima, Japan was destroyed with an atomic bomb, Major Bong died in the crash of a Lockheed Model P-80 jet fighter that he was testing for the U.S. Air Force.

Publisher: Not Indicated ■ Manufacturer: Curteich Color Art Creations ■ Type: Chrome
■ Postmark: Not Used ■ Value Index: E

THE MEMPHIS BELLE

The Boeing B-17 bomber "Memphis Belle" was the first bomber and crew to complete twenty-five bombing missions during World War II. It was returned to Memphis, TN in 1946 and displayed as shown in this photograph. On May 17, 1987, the "Memphis Belle" was enshrined in a new crested domed pavilion. The housing ceremony featured a fly-over by seven of the remaining approximately one dozen flyable B-17s.

Publisher: Card No. 68269-B, Thompson's Community Service, 1220 Chickasaw, Paris, TN
■ Manufacturer: Dexter Press, West Nyack, NY ■ Type: Chrome ■ Postmark: Not Used ■ Value Index: F

The "Memphis Belle" was actually Miss Margaret Polk, at one time the fiancee of Captain Robert Morgan, the B-17's pilot. She and most of the original crew members were present for the housing ceremonies.

A North American B-25 medium bomber is on display at the Milwaukee, Wisconsin Airport. The B-25 "Mitchell" bomber and Milwaukee's Mitchell Field were named in honor of Major General William L. "Billy" Mitchell, a native of Milwaukee and a pioneer of modern military aviation. This display was erected as a lasting tribute by the local Rotary Club.

As the number of remaining World War II aircraft becomes exceedingly small, many of those aircraft displayed in this manner are being retrieved for exhibition in museums for protection from vandalism and the elements.

Publisher: Card No. 1490-C, 353Z, The L.L. Cook Co. ■ Manufacturer: The L.L. Cook Company, Milwaukee, WI ■ Type: Chrome ■ Postmark: Not Used ■ Value Index: F

Publisher: Card No. DS-268, Deep South Specialties, Inc., P.O. Box 1802, Jackson, MS ■ Manufacturer: H.S. Crocker Co., Inc., San Francisco, CA ■ Type: Chrome ■ Postmark: Not Used ■ Value Index: F

This Vought-Sikorsky OS2U "Kingfisher" is shown on the deck of the battleship U.S.S. "Alabama", now serving as a war memorial at Mobile, Alabama. The aircraft was a gift from the Mexican Navy, and is the only assembled aircraft of its type on display in the United States. The restoration was accomplished by Brookley Air Force Base personnel during their off-duty hours. The hoist in the background was used to retrieve the "Kingfisher" after it had landed on the water and taxied along side of the ship.

Other aircraft on display at the Alabama Memorial are a North American P-51 "Mustang" and a Chance-Vought F4-U "Corsair".

Many new light plane designs made their appearance at the end of World War II hoping to capture the potential market of all the exmilitary flyers. This market did not develop as anticipated because of economic conditions and the fact that many exmilitary flyers were not enthusiastic about continuing their flying (many for economic reasons). As a result of these factors, only a few of these designs survived. One of the aircraft was this Stinson "Voyager-150" produced originally by the Stinson Division of Consolidated-Vultee Aircraft Corporation. A few were also assembled by Piper Aircraft Company in 1949.

Publisher: Not Indicated ■ Manufacturer: Not Indicated ■ Type: Black and White ■ Postmark: Not Used ■ Value Index: E

The "Voyager-150" is a version of the Model 108 series. It had the largest sales record as a four-place aircraft at the time. Many of these aircraft continue to fly today, a large number having had the original fabric covering on the fuselage replaced with metal for durability and longer life.

Publisher: Not Indicated ■ Manufacturer: J.P. Walmer, Box 224, Harrisburg, PA ■ Type: Linen ■ Postmark: Not Used ■ Value Index: D

The major post World War II offering of Piper Aircraft Company, the best known of all U.S. aircraft manufacturers, was their "Super Cruiser". This three-place aircraft of 100 HP was actually a refined version of their prewar "Cub Cruiser".

By May of 1948, the last of 3,800 "Super Cruisers" were delivered when it began losing out in favor of the newer four-place aircraft. The "Super Cruiser" was designated the PA-12 as Piper had dropped the "J" prefix (as in J-3 "Cub") in favor of the PA (for Piper Aircraft) beginning with the PA-11 ("Cub Special").

A leisurely round-the-world flight of 22,500 miles was made by two "Super Cruisers" in 1947 to prove the reliability of the American lightplane.

The New De Luxe AERONCA "CHIEF"
AERONCA AIRCRAFT CORP. — MIDDLETOWN, OHIO

PRINTED IN U. S. A.   KODACHROME BY GROENHOFF

A manufacturer's post-card showing a photo-graph of the 1946 "Chief" by the Aeronca Aircraft Corporation. To compete with the Piper Aircraft Company, Aeronca pro-duced the "Chief" with side-by-side seating for two persons. This aircraft was used primarily for sport flying by the week-end pilots. Also, its coun-terpart, the Aeronca "Champion" was a very similar aircraft except for the seating being arranged in tandem. The "Cham-pion" was primarily a train-ing airplane.

Practically all parts of the "Chief" and "Champion" except the fuselage were interchangeable which made for ease of produc-tion. The construction for both aircraft was the typi-

Publisher: Aeronca Aircraft Corporation, Middletown, OH ■ Manufacturer: Curteich, Chicago, IL ■ Type: Linen
■ Postmark: Not Used ■ Value Index: B

cal fabric covered tubing. With a 65 HP engine, the "Chief" cruised at 95 MPH. Either airplane could have been pur-chased for about $2,600 in 1947.

A FINER FASTER CESSNA 140
A snappy 90 horsepower Cessna 140 brings you shorter take-off, quicker climb, faster cruise, and greater quietness. And with this a lovely and luxurious interior... your guarantee of comfortable and enjoyable flying. You'll get a new conception of light plane flying in the Cessna 140 and its sister ship, the 120.

Cessna
AIRCRAFT CO.
WICHITA, KANSAS

Publisher: Cessna Aircraft Company, Wichita, KS ■ Manufacturer: Not Indicated ■ Type: Chrome
■ Postmark: Not Used ■ Value Index: B

An advertising postcard produced for the Cessna Aircraft Company. As with the Aeronca Company, Cessna's postwar offerings were the "120" with no frills, intended mostly for pilot training and the "140" with deluxe features such an an electrical system, starter, generator, and wing flaps. The "140" was more appealing to the sportsman pilot.

The only external difference was the side windows in the "140". Attractive features of both aircraft were the all-metal fuselages and a new maintenance-free, spring-steel landing gear. This latter feature was an invention of Mr. Steve Wittman, the racing pilot. The "140" was later produced with an all-metal wing and single wing strut and iden-tified as the "140A"

One of the most popular aerial shows was the Cole Brothers Airshow. Operated by the brothers, Duane, Lester, and Marion, they performed from 1946 through 1963.

This photograph shows a "Charky" the Stearman owned by Marion Cole flying inverted with a wing rider. This exmilitary trainer has been modified for airshow work by installing a larger 450 HP engine, fairings on the wheels, and a smoke system. The airshow smoke added color to the performance and also helped to define the maneuvers. It is created by inducing oil into the exhaust system of the airplane.

The postcard is signed by "Lloyd H. Stoner", one of the performers in the

Publisher: Not Indicated ■ Manufacturer: Not Indicated ■ Type: Real Photo ■ Postmark: Not Used ■ Value Index: A

airshow. Duane and Marion Cole continue to perform regularly in flying exhibitions at this time.

Publisher: E.A.A. Aviation Museum Foundation, Inc., Hales Corners, WI ■ Manufacturer: Not Indicated ■ Type: Chrome// Postmark: Not Used ■ Value Index: F

Two popular performers at the annual Experimental Aircraft Association convention at Oshkosh, WI are Messrs. Wayne Pierce and Bob Wagner. The modified former military primary trainers, shown in this picture, with their loud engines and bright paint schemes continue to be a versatile airshow aircraft. Unfortunately, their numbers are diminishing. Also, new designs are being developed specifically for airshow performance including the Stephens "Akro" and the Laser "200" monoplanes.

As shown in the photograph, these biplanes have a fixture mounted on the wing to support the wing rider during the loops and inverted maneuvers.

The Blue Angles are shown in this photograph flying the Grumman F-11-F "Tiger" aircraft. This U.S. Navy flight demonstration team was formed in 1946 flying the propeller driven Grumman F-6-F "Hellcat".

The Blue Angels emphasize the fact that their performance is not just a series of stunts, but are precision maneuvers that would be learned and used in the U.S. Naval Air Service. Their duty is public relations and to encourage U.S. Navy Flying Service enlistments. The Blue Angels are currently flying the F-18 McDonnell fighter aircraft. Their support aircraft for personnel and equipment is a Lockheed C-130 "Hercules".

Publisher: Rowe Distributing Company, Norfolk, VA ■ Manufacturer: T.B. Lusterchrome ■ Type: Chrome ■ Postmark: Not Used ■ Value Index: F

The Thunderbirds, flight demonstration team of the U.S. Air Force was formed in 1953 flying the straight-wing Republic F-84G "Thunderjet". Shortly after their formation, they switched to the swept-wing F-84F "Thunder-streak" aircraft. Their aircraft are routinely upgraded to those being flown by the Air Force tactical units.

Publisher: Fairchild-Hiller Company ■ Manufacturer: Not Indicated ■ Type: Chrome ■ Postmark: Not Used ■ Value Index: D

The duty as a pilot or support person with the Thunderbirds is on a voluntary basis. The mission of the Thunderbirds is to project a favorable image of the U.S. Air Force and to encourage enlistments. In addition to their normal routine, the Thunderbirds have a low-level set of maneuvers for use when restricted by a low cloud base. The aircraft currently used by the Thunderbirds is the F-16 fighter aircraft.

Publisher: Not Indicated ■ Manufacturer: Not Indicated ■ Type: Real Photo
■ Postmark: Wilkes Barre, PA, June 23, 1931 ■ Value Index: B

The most successful of the Pitcairn line of Autogiros was the PCA-2 shown in this photograph. Twenty-four of this model were built, beginning in 1930. Unlike the modern helicopter, the early autogiros had small wings to contain the ailerons. As the tilting-head type of rotor was developed to give lateral and longitudinal control, the wings were eliminated beginning with the PA-39. A conventional engine and propeller were also used as the rotor was not powered except to be rotated to about 115 RPM prior to take-off by a clutch arrangement from the engine.

The "Silverbrook" Autogiro was operated by the Horizon Company of Wilkes Barre, PA, producers of Silverbrook Coal. The following message is printed on the back of the postcard: "A reminder of your trip in the autogiro. When you look at it remember to burn Silverbrook Anthracite-the good Lehigh hard coal that doesn't clinker." The postcards were apparently distributed to the passengers who were carried two at a time in the front cockpit.

The pilot on these passenger hops was Mr. Fred W. "Slim" Soule, a veteran Pitcairn test pilot who later demonstrated the efficiency of the autogiro as a crop dusting machine. The only remaining flyable Pitcairn Autogiro is the PCA-2 originally owned by the Champion Spark Plug Company. It is currently owned and flown by Stephen Pitcairn, the son of Harold Pitcairn, the founder of the company.

This 1944 helicopter designed for reconnaissance and antisubmarine work had a useful load of 1,500 pounds. The U.S. Navy designation was Model HO2S-1. The earlier Sikorsky R-4B had been the first American quantity-produced helicopter with 130 built for the U.S. Air Force, HNS-1 for the U.S. Navy, and for the British as the "Hoverfly." This aircraft differed mainly from the Model R-5 shown in the photograph by having side-by-side seating rather than the tandem arrangement and was fabric covered.

The very first production helicopter had been the German Flettner FL-282, the only helicopter used operationally during World War II. In January 1946, the R-5 established an unofficial altitude record for helicopters at 21,000 feet, and in November of that year established a helicopter speed record of 107 MPH.

Publisher: The Collotype Company, Elizabeth NJ and NY ■ Manufacturer: Not Indicated ■ Type: Real Photo
■ Postmark: Bridgeport, CT, August 7, 1955 ■ Value Index: B

In December 1951, New York Airways became the third helicopter service certified to fly airmail, serving routes between LaGuardia, Kennedy, and Newark Airports. The first certified airline was Los Angeles Airways in 1947, and the second certified airline was Chicago Airways in 1949.

On July 8, 1952, New York Airways became the first helicopter line authorized for passenger service and began with service between the three New York-New Jersey airports and several outlying towns using the same Sikorsky S-55 Helicopters. These S-55s were replaced in April 1958 by the Vertol Model 44B Twin-Rotor aircraft shown in the photograph. The Model 44B had a cabin similar to a conventional airliner and could accommodate 15 passengers.

Publisher: Card No. 22659-B, New York Airways ■ Manufacturer: Not Indicated ■ Type: Chrome
■ Postmark: Not Used ■ Value Index: F

For a short time beginning in December 1965, New York Airways also flew a passenger route between Kennedy Airport and the roof of the Pan-Am Building in Manhattan. The trip required only seven minutes each; these seventeen daily flights cost $7.00 one way or $10.00 round trip. The latest aircraft used by New York Airways was the twin-turbine, Twin-Rotor Vertol 107. By the late 1960s, service was curtailed due to government subsidies being withdrawn.

The Sikorsky S-58 helicopter when in the U.S. Marine service was designated as the UH-34. One of the main functions of military helicopters has been the search and rescue operation.

The helicopter shown in this photograph is recovering the Mercury space capsule after having hoisted Commander Alan Shepard aboard, and will proceed to land on the carrier U.S.S. "Lake Champlain". The U.S. Navy helicopter in the background is photographing the historic event. Circling the operation in upper right corner of the photograph is a Navy Lockheed P2V patrol aircraft.

Publisher: Card No. 53501, Rowe Distributing Company, Norfolk, VA ■ Manufacturer: Not Indicated ■ Type: Chrome ■ Postmark: Not Used ■ Value Index: F

An early American all cargo air service was ACT (Air Cargo Transport) Corporation. Based at the Newark, New Jersey Airport, they flew a transcontinental route with a fleet of the Douglas "Sky-Vans" as shown in the photograph.

The shipment of freight by air was slow to develop due to the complexities of government certification, and the fixing of rate schedules. Air freight at this time consisted mostly of items of a perishable nature such as fruit, fish, and flowers. ACT remained in service only from 1945 to 1947.

Publisher: Not Indicated ■ Manufacturer: Not Indicated ■ Type: Sepia ■ Postmark: Not Used ■ Value Index: C

One of the early all cargo air services in the U.S. was begun by United Airlines on December 23, 1940. A scheduled flight was operated daily from New York City to Chicago, IL. Their regular "Mainliner" utilized the passenger space for up to 5,000 pounds of freight. This service was ended May 31, 1941. In 1943, United Airlines established an all cargo route between New York City and San Francisco, CA using Douglas DC-3 aircraft.

Publisher: United Airlines ■ Manufacturer: Not Indicated ■ Type: Chrome ■ Postmark: Los Angeles, CA, July 12, 1948 ■ Value Index: F

As strictly all-cargo airlines were in operation during 1947, United Airlines began using these Douglas DC-6s with their payload divided. They carried approximately 50 passengers and 5,500 pounds of freight.

Known as the "Guppy" series, several of these strange looking craft were developed by extensively modifying the basic Boeing Model 377 "Stratocruiser" Airframe. The first of these conversions was the "Pregnant Guppy" of 1962. In 1965, the Super Guppy", the second and largest of the series was first flown. This "Super Guppy" shown in this photograph has the entire nose section including the flight deck hinged to open for loading.

In 1970, there appeared the "Guppy-101", a turbo-propeller version of the "Mini Guppy" and with a swing nose section for loading. The latest was the "Guppy-201", the same as the "Guppy-101" except the vertical tail was made higher and more angular.

Publisher: Not Indicated ■ Manufacturer: Scenic South Card Company, Bessemer, AL ■ Type: Chrome ■ Postmark: Not Used ■ Value Index: E

The "Super Guppy", owned by Aero-Space Lines is operated under NASA contract for the transport of rocket components. The "Guppy-201" was used to airlift large preassembled sections of the McDonnell-Douglas DC-10 and wing assemblies of the Lockheed L-1011 "TriStar" Airliners.

The most successful of the scheduled all-cargo-airlines has been the Flying Tiger Line. Founded in June 1945 by Robert Prescott, a former member of General Chennault's Flying Tigers, it was originally known as the National Skyway Freight Corporation. The name was officially changed to the Flying Tiger Line Incorporated in February 1947.

The line's first aircraft were fourteen Budd RB-1 "Conestogas". This twin-engine, rear-loading craft was of all stainless steel construction. The Budd Company of Philadelphia, Pennsylvania had been a producer of railway cars using stainless steel. The "Conestogas" could carry 7,000 pounds over a 500 mile range at 150 MPH.

Publisher: The Flying Tiger Line, Inc. ■ Manufacturer: Not Indicated ■ Type: Chrome ■ Postmark: Not Used ■ Value Index: F

The fleet of aircraft has been continuously updated until today it includes a number of these Boeing 747 passenger airliners converted to air freighters. These aircraft can carry 200,000 pounds at 575 MPH for 3,500 miles.

Very few aircraft have been built originally as air freighters. Many passenger type aircraft have been converted for this purpose. They can usually be distinguished by their lack of passenger windows and the oversize cargo doors.

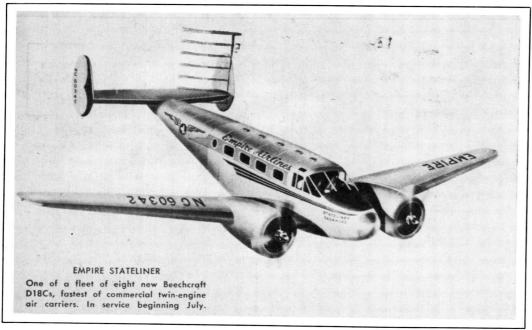

EMPIRE STATELINER
One of a fleet of eight new Beechcraft D18Cs, fastest of commercial twin-engine air carriers. In service beginning July.

Publisher: Not Indicated ■ Manufacturer: Not Indicated ■ Type: Black and White ■ Postmark: Buffalo, NY, November 13, 1946 ■ Value Index: D

The Beechcraft D-18C was a post World War II version of the popular "Twin-Beech" 18. It was certified as transport aircraft and more than 9,000 of the aircraft were produced beginning in 1937.

The Model D-18C, shown in this photograph, was intended for feeder airline use, however, it was not widely accepted. The best explanation for this lack of success was the availability of more economical exmilitary aircraft. Approximately 30 aircraft were manufactured. There were two principle differences from the earlier models, the larger Continental engines of 525 HP and the arrangement of the interior for the passengers.

Two of the aircraft were acquired by All-American Aviation for use on their airmail pickup system; this use did not prove practical. This aircraft was the first airliner to be equipped with a bird-proof windshield. It was tested by the Civil Aeronautics Authority by firing dead chickens at it.

Empire Airlines began operations in the Boise, ID area in 1946 using three Boeing 247D airliners, later using Douglas DC-3s and these Beechcraft D-18Cs. The Empire Airlines was absorbed by West Coast Airlines in August 1952.

Publisher: Central Airlines ■ Manufacturer: MWM Company, Aurora, MO ■ Type: Chrome ■ Postmark: Not Used
■ Value Index: D

The Consolidated-Vultee Model CV-240 "Convair" shown in this photograph has the markings of Central Airlines. It was the first of many models of this aircraft which were to follow. Carrying from 32 to 44 passengers it was ideal for the shorter flights of most airlines. It was initially placed into service by American Airlines in June 1948.

The aircraft that followed were the CV-340 and CV-440, both 4-1/2-feet longer and with improved engines providing a greater payload. This aircraft was later modified to accept the more powerful turbo-propeller engines. A large number were converted to turbine power such as the CV-580 with the Allison Engines and the Model CV-640 with Rolls-Royce Turbo Propellers.

A novel feature of the "Convairs" was the self-contained stairway that slid out from the fuselage just ahead of the wing. This feature provided quick handling of passengers. Some operators such as Western Airlines felt this arrangement was too close to the propellers and selected the retractable stairway at the rear of the fuselage below the tail surfaces.

Of the more than 400 military version aircraft that were delivered, many were converted to the T-29 for crew training and some to the C-131 transport.

The original Central Airlines merged with Pennsylvania Airlines in 1936 to become Penn-Central Airlines (PCA). A second Central Airlines began service in 1949 and was merged with Frontier Airlines in 1967.

Mohawk Airlines, a local service carrier began flying the "Convair 240" in 1955. Called the "Cosmopolitan" by Mohawk, one is shown in this photograph being overhauled in one of their two hangars, each hangar as large as a football field at the Oneida, NY County Airport. The permanent work dock permitted the maintenance men to reach all areas of the aircraft.

Mohawk was previously Robinson Airlines until the name change in August 1952. It was originally based in Ithaca, NY. In 1954, Mohawk became the first and only local service airline to operate scheduled helicopter flights. This service between the Newark, NJ Airport and Grossinger Field in the NY Catskill Mountains lasted only a few months as in-town heliports were not available to realize the benefits of helicopter travel.

Publisher: Not Indicated ■ Manufacturer: Hannau Color Productions, 475-5th Avenue, New York, NY ■ Type: Chrome ■ Postmark: Detroit, MI, August 23, 1959 ■ Value Index: D

The "Convair 440" was also operated by Mohawk from 1959 until 1966. Mohawk Airlines merged with Allegheny Airlines in 1971, and became part of the U.S. Air Airline.

A typical airport scene of the 1950s, in this photograph we see part of the Cleveland-Hopkins Airport, Cleveland, OH showing an assortment of piston-engine aircraft in use as airliners at that time. In clockwise order from the lower right, the aircraft are: A United Airlines "Convair" CV-340; a United Douglas DC-6; another United CV-340; an Eastern Airlines Martin 404; and, a Capital Airlines Lockheed "Constellation".

The airport traffic control tower may be seen at the far end of the concourse, near the top center of the photograph. The modern covered loading ramps that connect the terminal with the aircraft door were not available and passengers would be required to cross the open aircraft parking area to board their plane.

Publisher: George R. Klein News Company, Cleveland, OH ■ Manufacturer: Curteich, Chicago, IL ■ Type: Chrome ■ Postmark: Not Used ■ Value Index: F

A scaled-down version of the original three-rudder Douglas DC-4, acceptable to the airlines was flown in February 1942; however, production of the aircraft was diverted to the military services for the war effort. Approximately 1,160 were produced as the C-54 for the U.S. Air Corps and as the R5D for the U.S. Navy. It is estimated these aircraft made 79,642 ocean crossings during World War II and it was one of the main aircraft used in the Berlin Airlift.

As the war ended, many of the transports were converted back for airline use, such as the Colonial Airliner, shown in this photograph. Prior to May 1942, Colonial Arilines had been known as Canadian Colonial Airways. In June 1956, it was taken over by Eastern Airlines after completing 25 years of airline operations without a passenger fatality.

23 Colonial Airlines-Douglas DC-4

Publisher: Not Indicated ■ Manufacturer: Not Indicated ■ Type: Real Photo ■ Postmark: Not Used ■ Value Index: D

ONE OF CONTINENTAL'S NEW DOUGLAS DC—6B's

Publisher: Continental Airlines ■ Manufacturer: Curteich, Chicago, IL ■ Type: Linen ■ Postmark: Not Used ■ Value Index: E

The Douglas DC-6 series of aircraft were considered the first super transports of the postwar era. Although this aircraft had the same basic shape as the earlier DC-4, the Model DC-6 had a longer pressurized cabin and the more powerful Pratt & Whitney Double-Row Wasp Engines with 2,100 HP each, providing the aircraft with a normal cruising speed of 300 MPH.

The "B Model" of the DC-6 had the fuselage lengthened another five feet to accommodate 54 passengers on flights of average length or up to 90 passengers with a coach arrangement for shorter trips. The Douglas DC-6A was built as a freight carrying aircraft.

A specially equipped DC-6 became the personal aircraft for President Harry Truman, and was known as the "Independence". A C-54 (military DC-4) "The Sacred Cow" had been President Roosevelt's personal aircraft.

Varney Air Transport became Continental Airlines on July 1, 1937.

In 1942, Continental Airline began a scheduled military cargo service between San Francisco, California and Harrisburg, Pennsylvania.

An unusual photograph showing the view from a front angle of passengers deplaning from a Douglas DC-6B. A portable loading ranp is in use as these aircraft were not equipped with the self-contained stairway.

Northeast Airlines had ten of these Douglas DC-6Bs in their fleet during the late 1950s. The aircraft was designated the "Skylark" by Northeast Airlines. They were used on their routes linking New England with Florida. In 1968, their routes were extended to Bermuda and the Great Lakes. Northeast Airlines had evolved from Boston-Maine Airways on November 19, 1940, and was recently absorbed by Delta Airlines.

Publisher: Northeast Airlines ■ Manufacturer: Hannau Color Productions, 605 Lincoln Road, Miami Beach, FL ■ Type: Chrome ■ Postmark: Not Used ■ Value Index: B

Put into service in November 1953 by American Airlines, the Douglas DC-7 was a further development of the DC-6 series. The new aircraft was lengthened by eight feet over the DC-6 and used turbo-compound engines with four-bladed propellers. The cruising speed was 330 MPH.

The Douglas DC-7 had been built at the request of American Airlines who was seeking an aircraft to compete with the Lockheed Super Constellation of their rival, Trans-World Airlines. The DC-7 series made Transatlantic flights routine and profitable because of its increased payload and range. The DC-7C was the last of the series, and was forty inches longer than the DC-7.

Publisher: Mitock & Sons, 135611212 Ventura Blvd., Sherman Oaks, CA ■ Manufacturer: Colourpicture, Boston, MA ■ Type: Chrome ■ Postmark: Not Used ■ Value Index: D

The DC-7 shown in the photograph is preparing for takeoff from the Los Angeles, CA International Airport.

TWA Stratoliner in Flight   *TWA Color-foto*

Publisher: TWA ■ Manufacturer: American Colortype, Chicago, IL ■ Type: Chrome ■ Postmark: Not Used ■ Value Index: E

The Boeing 307 "Stratoliner" was America's first four-engined commercial aircraft with a pressurized passenger cabin. The same wing and similar tail surface assemblies of the B-17 bomber were used in construction of the 307.

As had occurred with several other large aircraft, after the test flying of the prototype, the engineers decided that additional vertical fin area was required. This modification was accomplished by reshaping the rudder and the fin to include a dorsal extension along the top of the fuselage.

This aircraft was the first land-based airliner to require the services of a flight engineer to eliminate some of the work load on the pilots. The first flight of the 307 was in December 1938, and only ten aircraft were built. Five of the aircraft were purchased by TWA and three aircraft were purchased by Pan-American Airways and designated "Stratoclippers".

One of the aircraft was acquired by Mr. Howard Hughes and fitted with a luxurious interior. It was known as the "Flying Penthouse". The tenth aircraft was lost in a crash while being test flown.

These airliners were drafted into military service during World War II and returned to TWA and Pan-Am in late 1944. They were flown by these airlines until 1951.

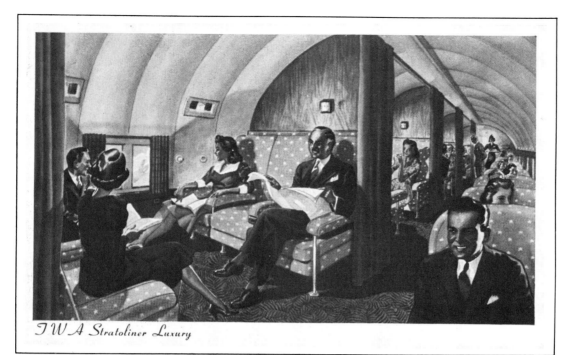

TWA Stratoliner Luxury

The luxurious cabin of the Boeing 307 "Stratoliner" was divided into four compartments, each seating six passengers on divan-type chairs. There was a single row of nine reclining chairs on the opposite side of the aisle. For use as a sleeper, the compartment divans were convertible to sixteen berths. With pressurization allowing the flight in the higher and smoother altitudes, these airliners were the most comfortable aircraft in service. Provision for passenger seat belts is not apparent in the photograph.

Although the wing of the Boeing B-17 bomber was used, the extra wide cabin (12 foot diameter) increased the overall span by 3-½ feet beyond the B-17.

Publisher: TWA ■ Manufacturer: American Colortype, Chicago, IL ■ Type: Chrome ■ Postmark: Not Used ■ Value Index: D

Northwest Airlines Stratocruisers   Coast To Coast...Hawaii...Alaska...Orient

The Boeing Model 377 "Stratocruiser" was derived from the military C-97 "Stratofreighter". Both designs usually used the wings, engines, and tail group of the wartime B-29 bomber and later changed to those of the post World War II B-50. A design change permitted the 38-foot high vertical fin to be folded down to a height of 26-½ feet for hangar clearance.

Publisher: Card No. PF16-A-49, Northwest Airlines ■ Manufacturer: Not Indicated ■ Type: Chrome ■ Postmark: Not Used ■ Value Index: D

The aircraft was capable of carrying up to 100 passengers, with a range of over 4,000 miles. This aircraft was the basic design from which the "Guppy" series was developed.

Although only 55 of the Boeing 377 "Stratocruiser" were purchased by five of the major airlines, they proved to be the most luxurious and popular aircraft until the introduction of the jet-powered fleet. Their double-deck configuration included a spiral stairway connecting the upper passenger deck to the lounge area and bar on the lower level. In service from 1949 until 1959, they flew many of the longer over-water routes, such as the Pan-American routes to Honolulu and Northwest to the Orient.

After being replaced by the newer jet aircraft on U.S. airlines, several of these aircraft were operated in Venezuela as cargo carriers until 1966. While Pan-American will prob-

Publisher: Pan-American World Airways ■ Manufacturer: Not Indicated ■ Type: Chrome ■ Postmark: Camden, AK, November 7, 1957 ■ Value Index: F

ably be best remembered for its giant flying boats, the last flight of which occurred in April 1946, they have been a successful operator since that time with a fleet consisting entirely of land-based aircraft.

Publisher: Not Indicated ■ Manufacturer: Cloos-Klozbucher, Frankfurt/Main, Foto: V.A.G. ■ Type: Real Photo ■ Postmark: Frankfurt/Main, Flughafen (Date Not Legible) ■ Value Index: D

The Lockheed "Constellation" Model 49, initially flown in January 1943 was the first in a long series of this design. As succeeding models were increased in size and new engines installed the gross weight increased from 90,000 pounds for the Model 49 to approximately 160,000 pounds for the final version, the Model 1649A "Starliner" in 1956.

Mr. Howard Hughes made large contributions in the designing of the "Constellation". He owned controlling interest in the TWA Airline during that time period. TWA and Pan-American were scheduled to receive the initial production of the "Constellations", however, as with the other new aircraft produced during this period, the initial production was taken over by the U.S. Army Air Forces and operated as the C-69 Military Transport.

In postwar operations, TWA used the "Connie" on its Transpolar Routes to Europe. In this photograph, wing-tip fuel tanks were installed on the aircraft as shown on this "Super G" Model 1649G at Frankfurt/Main Airport, Germany.

The graceful lines of the Lockheed "Constellation" aircraft distinguished it from all other airliners of the period. The airfoil shape of the fuselage was said to have contributed to the lift of the aircraft. Normal seating arrangement was for 64 passengers on daytime flights or 34 berths for the nighttime sleeper version.

SEEING IS BELIEVING
Eastern's New-Type Constellation demonstrating its amazing power—flying easily and smoothly on one of its 4 mighty engines. The world's most powerful and dependable airliner. Read other side.

Publisher: Eastern Airlines ■ Manufacturer: Not Indicated ■ Type: Chrome ■ Postmark: Washington, DC, August 22, 1949 ■ Value Index: F

Dependability of the airliner is emphasized in the text added to this photograph by Eastern Airlines showing flight on only one engine. Eastern was first to use the Model 1049 "Super Constellation" on December 7, 1951. This aircraft was 18 feet longer than the original model and had one-third more carrying capacity. Printed on back of the postcard is the statement, "Hand to flight attendant for mailing".

Chicago and Southern Air Lines 300 mph NEW *Luxury Constellation* built by Lockheed

Publisher: Chicago and Southern Air Lines ■ Manufacturer: Not Indicated ■ Type: Chrome ■ Postmark: Not Used ■ Value Index: D

Chicago and Southern Air Lines was the new name in 1934 after having been Pacific Seaboard Airlines. The airline began using the "Constellation" in 1948 on their routes that extended as far as Venezuela.

For additional cargo, the "Connie" could be fitted with a streamlined pod or "Speed-Pak" beneath the fuselage. This pod could be attached or disconnected readily at any stop on the route. With a capacity of four tons, the pod decreased the aircraft's speed by about ten MPH. Chicago and Southern Air Lines was merged with Delta Airlines in 1953.

Menu

CHILLED TOMATO JUICE
*FILET MIGNON WITH MUSHROOM GRAVY
WHIPPED POTATOES
BUTTERED GREEN BEANS
TOSSED GARDEN SALAD
WITH FRENCH DRESSING
ROLL AND BUTTER
HOT COFFEE. ICED TEA
FRESH STRAWBERRY SHORTCAKE
*FRIDAY BAKED SWORDFISH STEAK,
PIMIENTO BUTTER

1952

FLY Capital AIRLINES Constellations

THE LAST WORD IN LUXURY ALOFT

Publisher: Capital Airlines ■ Manufacturer: Not Indicated ■ Type: Chrome ■ Postmark: Washington, DC (Date Not Legible) ■ Value Index: D

With the long range of the modern aircraft such as the "Constellation", having meals in flight was becoming commonplace. Many of the airlines published postcards describing a typical menu as this postcard by Capital Airlines. Eleven Lockheed "Constellations" operated by Capital Airlines were sold when the airline was absorbed by United Airlines in 1961.

The best known of all "Constellations" was used by President Dwight D. Eisenhower during his period in office. Named the "Columbine", after the official flower of Mrs. Eisenhower's home state of Colorado, it was equipped with the most sophisticated communication and navigation equipment available at that time. All flights included a crew of eleven persons with a Lockheed Aircraft Technician.

In the 1960s, Capital International Airways became active as a Supplemental Air Carrier. The Supplemental Carriers were permitted to conduct unrestricted charter business; however, their scheduled services were limited to ten flights, one way, between any two cities per month.

The few "Constellations" remaining today are being utilized as restaurants or cocktail lounges. They are permanently parked at sites, similar to roadside diners.

The first American jet-powered aircraft was the Bell P-59 "Airocomet", test flown in October 1942. The German Heinkel HE-178 had flown in August 1939 and the British Gloster E.28/39 "Pioneer" was tested in May 1941. The "Airocomet" had twin engines of British design; they had been built in the United States by the General Electric Company. The rounded wingtips and tail surfaces on the prototype aircraft were squared off on production models as shown in this photograph.

Three 0.50-caliber machine guns and one 37mm cannon were installed in the nose. With a top speed of only 413 MPH and a tendency to sway from side to side, the P-59 was not acceptable as a fighter aircraft.

Publisher: Not Indicated ■ Manufacturer: Not Indicated ■ Type: Real Photo ■ Postmark: Not Used ■ Value Index: B

Approximately sixty aircraft were built and used for training purposes to acquaint the pilots who would be flying the future jet aircraft then being built. The first jet aircraft to be used in actual operational service was the German ME262 in 1944.

The first operational jet fighter used by the U.S. Air Force was the Lockheed P-80 "Shooting Star". Although it was delivered too late for World War II, the aircraft began service in December 1945 and was active in the Korean conflict.

The P-80 was slower and less maneuverable, with its straight wing, than the swept-wing Russian-built MIG-15; however, it was the victor against a MIG-15 in the world's first jet-fighter dog fight on November 8, 1950. The Russian straight wing fighters were not used in Korea. The swept-wing North American F-86 "Sabre" soon replaced the F-80 and proved to be more of a match for the MIG-15. (In 1948, the U.S. Air Force designations were changed from 'P' for Pursuit to 'F' for Fighter.)

Publisher: Texacolor Card Company ■ Manufacturer: H.S. Crocker Company, Inc., San Francisco, CA ■ Type: Chrome ■ Postmark: Wichita Falls, TX, September 7, 1951 ■ Value Index: B

An extensively modified "Shooting Star", now in the U.S. Air Force Museum, set a world speed record of 623.8 MPH in June 1947. Also in 1947, the TF-80C two-seat trainer version was built. In production this aircraft was known as the T-33 which became more popular than the fighter. Approximately 6,000 were built and used by more than twenty countries for various operations. Several of the T-33 trainers are being flown by civilians today.

The giant Consolidated B-36 intercontinental bomber never saw combat, but it was considered a major deterrent to aggression in the late 1940s and 1950s. Originally powered by six piston-pusher engines, the later Model B-36D also included four turbo-jet engines. Sixteen 20mm cannon in eight turrets were remotely controlled from two stations. Crew members moved between these stations by means of a wheeled dolly. All gun turrets except the nose and tail positions were retractable. The B-36 with a full load of bombs could remain in the air for twenty-four hours without refueling.

Publisher: Paul B.Lowney Photo Publishing Company, 532 14th Avenue, Seattle, WA ■ Manufacturer: Not Indicated ■ Type: Chrome ■ Postmark: Kings Beach, CA, August 20, 1956 ■ Value Index: B

The Model B-36 first flew in August 1946, and one of the last flights was that of the Model B-36 delivered to the U.S. Air Force Museum in April 1959. The wingspan of this aircraft was 230 feet.

The little known "Convair" YB-60 jet bomber first flew on April 18, 1952. It was developed from the "Convair" B-36 piston-engine bomber and its construction utilized a large number of B-36 components. The aircraft was intended to perform the same duties as the Boeing B-52 bomber. The eight Pratt & Whitney Jet Engines used in the YB-60 were similar to those powering the B-52.

Publisher: Texacolor Card Company ■ Manufacturer: H.S. Crocker Company, Inc., San Francisco, CA ■ Type: Chrome ■ Postmark: Grandview, TX, August 2, 1957 ■ Value Index: A

The aircraft wingspan of 206 feet was 21 feet longer than the B-52. The maximum speed was just over 500 MPH compared to 650 MPH for the B-52. The aircraft was never put into production, and only two prototypes were built.

Publisher: Chase Aircraft Company, Inc. ■ Manufacturer: Dexter Press, Pearl River, NY ■ Type: Black and White ■ Postmark: Not Used ■ Value Index A

The Chase XC-123 was the first aircraft known to have performed as a glider, a piston-powered transport, and a jet aircraft. The glider version, known as the XCG-20 was contracted on December 2, 1946. It was of all metal construction and a wingspan of 110 feet. The glider could carry 60 troops or 50 litter patients. Only one was completed. The first aircraft became the piston-powered XC-123, the second aircraft was converted to the jet XC-123A. Three hundred of the piston-powered aircraft were manufactured by the Fairchild Aircraft Company, and were known as the C-123 "Provider".

The Model C-123K with two General Electric Jet Engines each with 2,850 pounds of thrust was used in Vietnam as a short range and assault transport. The C-123A with jet power was the first American developed jet transport aircraft. It was not placed into production.

In 1964, the General Dynamics F-111A became the first production combat aircraft with variable sweep wings. On takeoff and at low speed, the wings are extended and at high speed the wings are swept back for maximum performance. The Defense Department was seeking a single tactical fighter for both the U.S. Navy and the U.S. Air Force in the F-111. However, the aircraft was not acceptable to the U.S. Navy because it was too large and heavy for use on aircraft carriers.

Publisher: Card No. 9112, Strykers' Western Fotocolor, 4604 E. Lancaster, Forth Worth, TX
■ Manufacturer: Anchor Color, Forth Worth, TX ■ Type: Chrome ■ Postmark: Not Used ■ Value Index: E

The Fairchild A-10 is the first U.S. Air Force aircraft specifically developed for the close air support of friendly ground forces. Its 30mm cannon is the most powerful gun ever installed in an aircraft. Eight tons of bombs can be carried at over 500 MPH. The engines are mounted to the rear for maximum protection from ground fire. Its ungainly appearance would seem to confirm the adage that given enough power, you can get a barn door to fly.

Publisher: Card No. 27397-D, Fairchild Industries ■ Manufacturer: Dexter Press, West Nyack, NY ■ Type: Chrome
■ Postmark: Not Used ■ Value Index: E

The Lockheed C-5 "Galaxy" of 1970 was at that time the world's largest aircraft. Designed to airlift and also airdrop all types of heavy combat and support equipment, it could carry 100 tons over 3,000 miles or lesser amounts over 5,000 miles. Its twelve wing tanks can hold 49,000 gallons of fuel. Other impressive specifications include: a wingspan of 223 feet; a length of 242 feet; and, tail height of 63 feet.

Publisher: Card No. 131400, Charleston Post Card Company, Photo by Ernest Ferguson ▪ Manufacturer: Not Indicated ▪ Type: Chrome ▪ Postmark: Not Used ▪ Value Index: F

Publisher: E.A.A. Aviation Foundation, Franklin, WI ▪ Manufacturer: Not Indicated ▪ Type: Chrome ▪ Postmark: Not Used ▪ Value Index: F

The restoration of antique aircraft has enjoyed a resurgence for the pilots who enjoy their sport flying in an open cockpit. This 1928 Pitcairn is a good example. The PA-5 "Sport Mailwing" shown in this photograph was the sport plane version of the standard "Mailwing". A two-place front cockpit replaced the mail compartment. This aircraft was originally the personal airplane of Mr. Harold Pitcairn, the Company founder. The aircraft is currently owned and flown by his son, Mr. Stephen Pitcairn. Other examples of the Pitcairn "Mailwing" may be seen in the National Air and Space Museum, the Virginia Aviation Museum, and the Old Rhinebeck Aerodrome in New York.

Another antique aircraft finding favor with restorers who desire an enclosed cabin is the three-place 1929 Curtiss "Robin". The "Robin" shown in this photograph is powered with a Continental Engine of 220 HP. Originally, the airplane came equipped with the Curtiss OX-5 water-cooled engine of 90 HP, or the six-cylinder radial Curtiss "Challenger" engine of 170 HP. The "Challenger" engine was one of only a very few radial engines built with an even number of cylinders; another was the Curtiss "Chieftan" with two rows of six cylinders each.

The "Robin" could be purchased with the narrow stream-lined steel-tube wing struts or the wider airfoil lifting-struts similar

1929 Curtiss Robin   Cabin Monoplane

Publisher: Card No. 122078, Ackerson, P.O. Box 23, Slate Hill, NY ■ Manufacturer: Not Indicated ■ Type: Chrome ■ Postmark: Not Used ■ Value Index: E

to those used on the Bellanca monoplanes. Several Curtiss "Robins" were used in the early endurance record flights and the record of 27 days established in 1935 by the Key Brothers flying the Robin "Ole Miss" remains unbeaten today for single-engine aircraft. The "Ole Miss" is now in the National Air and Space Museum.

For the people who prefer to do their sport flying in a more modern aircraft, the Beechcraft "Musketeer" is one of the few light aircraft to be produced in recent years.

The models shown in the photograph (from top to bottom) are the two-seat "Sport" and the four-seat "Custom" and "Super". Engine power increases (in that order) from 150 HP to 180 HP for the "Custom" and 200 HP for the "Super". Cruising speeds vary from 131 MPH for the "Sport" to 143 MPH and 150 MPH for the "Custom" and "Super".

Similar Beechcraft models are the "Sundowner" and the "Sierra" which has a retractable landing gear. The Beechcraft "Sport" is a popular aircraft for civilian

Publisher: Beech Aircraft Corporation, Wichita, KS ■ Manufacturer: Not Indicated ■ Type: Chrome ■ Postmark: Not Used ■ Value Index: E

pilot training. The Beechcraft Company had a greater reputation for the "V" tail "Bonanza" and their twin-engine business aircraft.

Another modern aircraft that is popular with the sport flyer is the Cessna Model 152. This two-seater of high-wing design is also widely used as a training airplane. The Cessna line of personal airplanes includes a number of aircraft similar to the "152" with seating for four people. The aircraft include the "Cardinal", "Skyhawk", and "Skylane". Some of these aircraft have turbo-propeller engines and retractable landing gear. Their twin-engine models include the unique twin-boom "Skymaster" with tractor and pusher engines.

Publisher: Cessna Aircraft Company, Wichita, KS ■ Manufacturer: Not Indicated ■ Type: Chrome ■ Postmark: Not Used ■ Value Index: F

The debut of the turbine-powered airliner was made in 1955 when Capital Airlines introduced the British-built "Vickers Viscount" shown in this photograph. This aircraft is one of several types of turbo-propeller airliners that provided economical operation for many airlines moving into the jet era which began in late 1958. Capital purchased sixty of these forty-eight passenger airliners. It was the first British transport to be used in substantial numbers by America's airlines.

The turbo-propeller engine is basically a jet engine driving a propeller for improved efficiency at lower speeds and altitudes. A reduction gear is employed to reduce the high speed of the turbine to a more practical RPM for the propeller.

Publisher: George R.Klein News Company, Cleveland, OH ■ Manufacturer: Curteich Color Art-Creation ■ Type: Chrome ■ Postmark: Not Used ■ Value Index: F

The "Viscount" in the photograph shows passengers boarding the aircraft at the Cleveland-Hopkins Airport. The control tower is in the center background.

Another turbo-propeller aircraft was the Fokker "Friendship" built by the Dutch. Although the aircraft was initially test flown in 1955, it did not go into regular airline service until September 1958. West Coast Airlines purchased the aircraft that were built under license by the Fairchild Aircraft Company of Hagerstown, MD and known as the F-27. One of the aircraft is shown in the photograph over the Golden Gate Bridge. Intended as a replacement for the aging DC-3, the initial cost and high operating cost did not permit this aircraft to achieve that position.

It was utilized by several other local carriers including Bonanza, Pacific, Ozark, and Piedmont,

Publisher: West Coast Airline ■ Manufacturer: H.S. Crocker Company, Inc., San Francisco, CA ■ Type: Chrome ■ Postmark: Not Used ■ Value Index: E

however, the majority of the airlines chose to continue using the "Convairs" and Martin aircraft. The design continued to have favorable operating conditions in many other parts of the world and production continued into 1981. The aircraft had maximum passenger appeal because of its high-wing design that permitted easier boarding and better visibility.

The first and only American built turbo-propeller aircraft to have regular commercial airline service was the Lockheed Model L-188 "Electra". The aircraft was test flown in December 1957 and it entered airline service in January 1959. Within approximately one year from the time of beginning service, this aircraft had two accidents. In each case, the cause was an unknown "Whirl Anode" dynamic condition in which propeller motions coupled with wing deflections to produce wing failure. After a lengthy period of modifications by Lockheed, during which time the remaining aircraft were operated at reduced speed and altitude, they were returned to service and performed as originally intended.

NORTHWEST *Orient* AIRLINES L. R. LOCKHEED ELECTRA/JET

Publisher: Northwest Orient Airlines ■ Manufacturer: Not Indicated ■ Type: Chrome ■ Postmark: Not Used ■ Value Index: F

The first of Northwest's 80 passenger, 400 MPH "Electras" began service in September 1959. As shown on the photograph, the word "Jet" was interpreted loosely as the "Electra" is actually a turbo-propeller powered aircraft. The U.S. Navy's Lockheed P-3A "Orion" is derived from the commercial "Electra" and it became the U.S. Navy's principle long-range reconnaissance aircraft.

One of the last airline turbo-propeller aircraft was the Fairchild-Hiller F-227, an enlarged version of the F-27. The aircraft was introduced by Mohawk Airlines in July 1966. One of these aircraft is shown loading passengers at Warren County Airport, Glens Fall, NY.

Externally, it could be distinguished from the F-27 by the two additional

Publisher: Dean Color, Glens Falls, NY ■ Manufacturer: Dexter Press, Inc., West Nyack, NY ■ Type: Chrome
■ Postmark: Not Used ■ Value Index: E

sets of cabin windows located ahead of the propellers. Two turbo-props of foreign manufacture to make their appearance in small numbers were the French "Nord" 262 and the Japanese "Nihon" YS-11A. The era of the turbo propeller was relatively short with the ideal aircraft never having been developed. The smaller airlines had to wait for the arrival of the small all-jet airliner.

Of the short-to-medium range jetliners, there were four types with rear-mounted engines considered as the most prominent. The first of these aircraft was the French Sud-Aviation "Caravelle". When the "Caravelle" entered service with United Airlines in July 1961, it was the first foreign jet transport to be utilized by a U.S. airline.

To expedite construction, the nose section of the British DeHaviland "Comet" was used. The aircraft was powered by two Rolls-Royce Engines of 11,400 pounds thrust each. Eighty passengers could be carried 1,000 miles at 450 MPH. The aircraft was known for its quietness and the triangle-shaped, stress-resistant windows

Publisher: United Airlines ■ Manufacturer: Not Indicated ■ Type: Chrome ■ Postmark: Not Used
■ Value Index: F

were a distinctive external feature. A total of 280 aircraft were manufactured.

FLY MOHAWK
The First Airline in the East with ONE-ELEVEN fan-jet service!

Publisher: Mohawk Airlines ■ Manufacturer: Not Indicated ■ Type: Chrome ■ Postmark: Not Used ■ Value Index: F

Another foreign built short-range airliner was the British Aircraft Corporation BAC-111, similar in appearance to the "Caravelle", except for the 'T' tail arrangement. It was also a slightly smaller aircraft with a passenger capacity of 65 and a range of approximately 900 miles. American, Braniff, and Mohawk Airlines were using this aircraft in 1965-66.

The Boeing Model 727, similar in size to the French "Caravelle" was improved in performance because a third engine was installed in the tail cone. This aircraft was placed in service in February 1964 by Eastern Airlines. Also, the 727 was flown by Northwest Airlines. As a result of this usage, it became the world's best selling jet airliner. Records indicate

The Boeing 727 — newest addition to Northwest's Fan-Jet Fleet

Publisher: Northwest Orient Airlines ■ Manufacturer: Not Indicated ■ Type: Chrome ■ Postmark: Not Used ■ Value Index: F

1,825 were ordered by the end of 1981. Originally designed for 120 passengers, by lengthening the fuselage and adding more powerful engines later aircraft such as the 727-200 could seat 178.

The 727 was known for its sophisticated arrangement of wing flaps and slots enabling the airfoil shape to be regulated for both high cruising speeds and for relatively short takeoff and landing capabilities.

The Douglas Aircraft Company offering for the medium-range routes was their Model DC-9, very similar to the BAC-111 with an equal wingspan and a longer fuselage permitting the carrying of additional passengers. The first aircraft in service were the Delta Airlines original 90-seat version in December 1965. Southern Airways began their DC-9 service in June 1967.

Numerous models were in continuous development through 1980, when the Super 80 series was flown. These aircraft were capable of carrying 172 passengers. The rear mounting of the engines had proved to have several advantages, including an aerodynamically clean wing surface, the engines were easier to maintain, and the cabin was exceptionally quiet. Southern Airways was merged with Frontier Airlines on October 1, 1967.

Publisher: Southern Airways, Inc. ■ Manufacturer: Not Indicated ■ Type: Chrome ■ Postmark: Not Used ■ Value Index: E

Publisher: Continental Airlines ■ Manufacturer: Curteich Color Reproductions ■ Type: Chrome ■ Postmark: Chenoa, IL, September 18, 1959 ■ Value Index: E

As the long-range jet fleet developed in the late 1950s and early 1960s, the aircraft were dominated by three manufacturers. Each aircraft had four wing-mounted engines. The first and most well-known aircraft was the Boeing Model 707 shown in the photograph with Continental Airlines markings. The first version of the aircraft was produced as the Air Force KC-135 "Strato-tanker". Commercial use of the 707 was begun in late 1958 on the Pan-American Airways New York to Paris route. In early 1959, the Boeing 707 was used by American Airlines for the first Transcontinental jet service.

It is often difficult to define the specifications for particular models of the aircraft, as quantities for certain airlines were tailored to their specific requirements. These changes included seating arrangement and the type of engine. The choice of an engine will determine the performance characteristics. The scope of Continental Airlines' operations was greatly expanded recently by their acquisition of People's Express Airline.

Publisher: Trans-Caribbean Airways ■ Manufacturer: Not Indicated ■ Type: Chrome ■ Postmark: Not Used ■ Value Index: F

Nearly identical to the Boeing 707 in configuration, but slightly larger was the Douglas DC-8. The most apparent differences from the 707 were the thinner fuselage and the narrower vertical fin. Doulgas DC-8s were the first jets to be operated by Eastern Airlines.

When production ceased in 1972, 556 aircraft comprising various models of the Douglas DC-8 had been built. Trans Caribbean Airways, whose DC-8 is shown in this photograph was acquired by American Airlines in December 1970.

The "Convair" CV-990, though similar in appearance to the Boeing 707 and the Douglas DC-8, could be distinguished by the four tapered wing fairings which improved speed and stability and also were used as fuel tanks. As shown in the photograph, this model was developed for American Airlines. Performance of the aircraft was not as guaranteed,

Publisher: American Airlines ■ Manufacturer: Not Indicated ■ Type: Chrome ■ Postmark: Not Used ■ Value Index: E

and all of the Model CV-990 aircraft were given a series of modifications to improve speed and range at great expense to the manufacturer; it emerged as the 990A. Only 37 of the 990 aircraft were produced. The Company records indicate 65 of the smaller preceding Model CV-880 were built. Delta Airlines was one of the major users of the smaller aircraft.

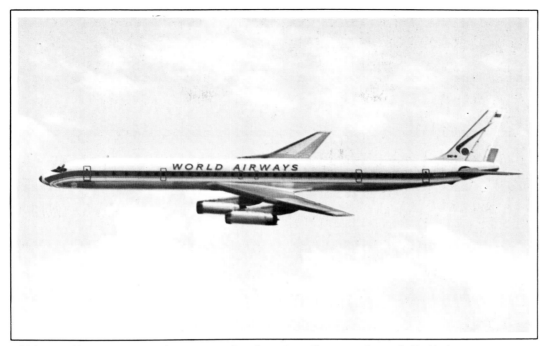

Publisher: World Airways ■ Manufacturer: Not Indicated ■ Type: Chrome ■ Postmark: Not Used
■ Value Index: F

The practice of stretching an aircraft of proven design was becoming commonplace. In many cases, by elongating the fuselage and adding more powerful engines the payload and performance could be increased significantly. An extreme example of this change is the World Airways DC-8 "Super Stretch" with the fuselage lengthened by 37 feet. A freighter version of the "Super Stretch" series was used by the Flying Tiger Freight Line.

Publisher: United Airlines ■ Manufacturer: Not Indicated ■ Type: Chrome ■ Postmark: Not Used
■ Value Index: F

At the end of the 1960s, a new class of wide body or "Jumbo" airliners was beginning to appear. The largest of these aircraft was the Boeing Model 747. This United Airlines 747-100 is the original version with accommodations for nearly 400 passengers in eight-abreast seating. A freighter model with a hinged nose for loading, to carry more than 257,000 pounds, is also available. To support this weight while the aircraft is on the ground, a landing gear assembly of 18 wheels is used.

The aircraft was test flown in February 1969. The 747 was initially placed in service on Pan-American's New York to London route in January 1971. Some of the interesting specifications include a wingspan of 195 feet, length of 231 feet, height at 63 feet, and gross weight 710,000 pounds.

The second wide-body jet liner to enter service was the Tri-Jet McDonnell-Douglas DC-10. It has two engines on the wings and one in the tail. Somewhat smaller than the Boeing 747, it could accommodate between 250 and 350 passengers depending on the cabin layout.

This Continental Airlines DC-10-30 shown in the photograph, is an extended range model meant for intercontinental use. This view of the aircraft in landing attitude shows the third set of wheels fitted to the DC-10-30 model.

Publisher: Continental Airlines, Photo by John D. Clayton ■ Manufacturer: Not Indicated ■ Type: Chrome ■ Postmark: Not Used ■ Value Index: F

Publisher: Delta Airlines ■ Manufacturer: Not Indicated ■ Type: Chrome ■ Postmark: Not Used ■ Value Index: G

A third wide-body type was the Lockheed L-1011, "TriStar", also a three-engine aircraft. Production of the L-1011 was delayed considerably by the bankruptcy of the engine maker, Rolls-Royce of England in February 1971 and the poor financial status of the Lockheed Company. The Rolls-Royce Company was eventually reorganized and controlled by the British Government and emergency loans were granted to Lockheed by the U.S. Government enabling the L-1011 to enter scheduled service with Eastern Airlines in April 1972.

A legend on back of this Delta Airlines postcard states, "The 302 passenger airplane has a cruising speed of over 550 MPH and a range of over 2475 statute miles. Three pilots and nine flight attendants make up the Tristar crew."

A much smaller jet liner for the short-medium range routes is the Boeing Model 737. The wide body appearance is due to the fuselage being of the same cross section as the much larger 707. Sales of the 737 were sluggish for several years when the Airline Pilot Association (ALPA) insisted on a three-man crew in the cockpit. Many smaller airlines could not accept the additional operating expense for a third crew member. ALPA agreed to a two-man crew in 1974.

This Southwest Airlines 737-200, as shown in the photograph, is six feet longer than the original 737-100.

Publisher: Southwest Airlines ■ Manufacturer: Not Indicated ■ Type: Chrome ■ Postmark: Not Used ■ Value Index: F

While the U.S. aircraft industry was supplying most of the world's airliner fleets, it had neglected to come up with a new design aircraft for the expanding short-haul commuter airlines. Consequently, in the mid 1960s, the U.S. commuter fleet was beginning to include many foreign built aircraft. One of the first aircraft in use was the French-built "Nord" 262 shown in the photograph. It was a 28-seat, twin turbo-propeller aircraft operated by Ransome Airlines, part of the Allegheny Commuter System. Another user of the aircraft was Lake Central Airlines which in March 1968 merged with Allegheny Airlines.

Publisher: Ransome Airlines ■ Manufacturer: Not Indicated ■ Type: Chrome ■ Postmark: Nokesville, VA, August 2, 1972 ■ Value Index: E

Publisher: Merchandising Distributors, P.O. Box 2127, Littleton, CO ■ Manufacturer: Not Indicated ■ Type: Chrome
■ Postmark: Not Used ■ Value Index: E

Another foreign built aircraft in wide use in the U.S. Commuter Lines is the Canadian built De-Haviland DHC-7, a four-engine, 50-passenger aircraft. This aircraft, shown in this photograph, is known for its ability to take off and land in very short distances, for the fuel efficient engines, and the quietness of operation, especially when taking off and landing. This latter feature is very important among the many noise-sensitive communities. Prior to late 1968, Rocky Mountain Airways had been known as Vail Airways.

Publisher: Jonas Aircraft Company ■ Manufacturer: Dexter Press, West Nyack, NY ■ Type: Chrome
■ Postmark: Not Used ■ Value Index: D

For the very short commuter routes, the British built Britten-Norman BN-2A "Islander" was available. This twin-engine aircraft with seating for nine passengers is shown in the photograph being used by Princeton Airways for their flights between the Princeton and Newark, NJ Airports. Operations of this type are taking the place of expensive and time consuming ground transportation in congested areas of the country. The Britten-Norman "Trislander" with a third engine mounted in the vertical fin is also used for these short commuter operations.

This unusual looking aircraft is considered to be the world's first wide body commuter airliner. The United Kingdom built "Shorts" Model SD3-30 can carry thirty passengers in wide body comfort. The factory is located in Belfast, Northern Ireland.

Golden West Airlines, operating in California, assumed its present format in 1969 with the acquisition of several small commuter lines. Another U.S. operator of the "Shorts" SD3-30 is Mississippi Valley Airlines.

Publisher: Not Indicated ■ Manufacturer: Multiple Photos, Los Angeles, CA ■ Type: Chrome ■ Postmark: Not Used ■ Value Index: F

Publisher: Cessna Aircraft Company, Wichita, KS ■ Manufacturer: Not Indicated ■ Type: Chrome ■ Postmark: Not Used ■ Value Index: F

Reflecting the advancement in aircraft design since the development of Mr. Clyde Cessna's first aircraft is this modern twin-engine Cessna "Conquest" shown flying over the City of St. Louis. The "Conquest" has a range of 2,625 miles, cruising at 337 MPH. The "Citation", a twin jet business aircraft is also produced by the Cessna Company.

Where a corporate aircraft of larger capacity is required, this "Gulfstream IV" can carry eight passengers and baggage, plus a crew of three nonstop over 5,000 miles. Built by the Grumman Aircraft Company, the "Gulfstream" is the most popular of the larger business jet aircraft. The vertical winglets at the wingtips are a recent aerodynamic innovation that improves the general performance and greatly increases fuel efficiency.

Publisher: Gulfstream Aerospace Corporation, P.O. Box 2206 Savannah, GA ■ Manufacturer: Not Indicated
■ Type: Chrome ■ Postmark: Not Used ■ Value Index: E

Probably the most well-known of all light aircraft is the Piper "Cub". Originally the Taylor "Cub" as designed by Mr. C.G. Taylor, it became the Piper "Cub" in 1937 when the company moved from Bradford, PA to Lock Haven, PA and changed its name when Taylor left the company. Over 14,000 of these aircraft were built, the last in 1947, with engines of 40 to 65 HP.

The majority of the flight schools in the wartime Civilian Pilot Training Program were equipped with the Piper "Cub" aircraft. For solo flight, the "Cub" was rigged to be flown from the rear of the tandem seats. Mr. C.G. Taylor went on to establish the Taylorcraft Company which produced a popular

1945 PIPER CUB J-3 TRAINER

Publisher: Not Indicated ■ Manufacturer: Not Indicated ■ Type: Chrome ■ Postmark: Not Used
■ Value Index: E

aircraft with that name. The aircraft was very similar to the "Cub", but with side-by-side seating. The 1945 model shown in this photograph is part of the Shannon Air Museum at Fredricksburg, VA. Most of these museum aircraft have recently been relocated to the Virginia Aviation Museum in Richmond, VA.

118

In recent years, the number of home-built aircraft has nearly kept pace with the production of factory-built aircraft. This movement has been encouraged by the Experimental Aircraft Association.

Designed by Mr. Paul H. Poberezny, the president of the Association, the "Acro-Sport" shown in the photograph is a favorite among the homebuilders of aircraft. Its early open-cockpit biplane design combined with the use of modern engine and materials provides an ideal home-type project. The aircraft is capable of performing almost unlimited aerobatics.

Publisher: Card No. 42940-D, Times Publishing Company, 453 Fifth Street, Random Lake, WI, Photo by Dick Stouffer.
■ Manufacturer: Not Indicated ■ Type: Chrome ■ Postmark: Not Used ■ Value Index: E

Publisher: E.A.A. Aviation Museum Foundation, Inc., Hales Corners, WI, Photo by Jack Cox
■ Manufacturer: Not Indicated ■ Type: Chrome ■ Postmark: Not Used ■ Value Index: E

A unique aircraft design popular with the homebuilders of aircraft is the "Vari-Eze". Developed by Mr. Burt Rutan, the designer of the "Around-The-World-Voyager", it uses the latest technology and materials with most of the contruction utilizing foam and fiberglass.

The two-place pusher design has proven to be a very practical cross-country aircraft. This group of the aircraft at the Oshkosh, WI Experimental Aircraft Association Convention are positioned with the nose wheel retracted for ease of entry into the aircraft. The short canard surface (wing) at the nose is not considered a new idea as it has been used on some of the earliest aircraft.

The Warbirds of America is a division of the Experimental Aircraft Association (EAA). Its members restore and maintain exmilitary aircraft in their original condition. All types of aircraft are involved, from the light-liaison types to the multiengine bombers.

The photograph shows a small section of the Warbirds area at the annual EAA Convention at Oshkosh, WI. The aircraft are mostly the North American AT-6 and SNJ Advanced Trainers. These aircraft are the most plentiful and more economical to operate than the fighters and bomber types. The Warbirds perform in the daily airshows at the Oshkosh Convention with demonstrations of combat tactics and formation flying.

Publisher: Card No. 0133-870844, K & A Petersen, 1948 S. 50 E., Orem, UT, Photo by Allardice
■ Manufacturer: Not Indicated ■ Type: Chrome ■ Postmark: Not Used ■ Value Index: E

The annual convention of the Experimental Aircraft Association (EAA) at Oshkosh, WI has become the world's largest aviation event. Its main purpose is to encourage, promote, and help to preserve all facets of personal flying. Hundreds of educational forums and seminars are conducted on aircraft and flying wih the emphasis on safety.

Publisher: Card No. 176925, K & A Petersen, 1948 So. 50 E., Orem, UT, Photo by Allardice ■ Manufacturer: Not Indicated ■ Type: Chrome ■ Postmark: Not Used ■ Value Index: E

The thousands of aircraft that are flown in to the Convention make Oshkosh the busiest airport in the country for the week. The small portion of the Convention shown in the photograph is a part of the Antique and Classic Aircraft Area. A World Class Aviation Museum open all year to the public is also maintained at the Oshkosh site.

The supersonic transport "Concorde" was a joint project of the British Aircraft Corporation (BAC) and the French Sud Aviation Company (later Aerospatiale). The design was begun in 1962, the first test flight was not made until 1969. Plagued by many design problems and high operating costs, the aircraft was finally put into service in 1976 by the national airlines of the two countries, British Airways and Air France.

AM719   CONCORDE   G-BOAC   1975
(By Courtesy of British Airways)

Pamlin Prints
Croydon CRO 1HW

Publisher: British Airways ■ Manufacturer: Pamlin Prints, Croydon CRO 1HW, England ■ Type: Black and White ■ Postmark: Not Used ■ Value Index: E

Flights were not made into the U.S. until late 1977 due to a ban on supersonic flight and opposition to the noise of the aircraft. Production was halted in 1979 after sixteen aircraft had been built. At the beginning of 1982, each airline had seven aircraft in use. With 34,000 gallons of fuel in its wing tanks a New York to Paris flight at 50,000 feet requires three hours and forty-five minutes. The speed is approximately 1,350 MPH. Typical seating arrangements are for 100 passengers.

Publisher: Card No. 134495, M. Landre, 455 Woodland Street, Merritt Island, FL ■ Manufacturer: Not Indicated ■ Type: Chrome ■ Postmark: Not Used ■ Value Index: F

The U.S. SST program was cancelled after the building of a full size mock-up of the aircraft by the Boeing Airplane Company. This 288-foot long design was intended to carry 300 persons at 1,800 MPH. The aircraft is shown in the artist's rendition. There was strong public opposition to the aircraft for environmental and economic reasons. In May 1971, government funds which had financed the project were no longer awarded. The mock-up which had cost several million dollars to construct was sold at auction for approximately $30,000, and was placed on display at the SST Exhibit Center near Kissimmee, FL.

Bibliography

The following books and publications were used as sources of information in preparing this book:
Allen, Oliver E., THE AIRLINE BUILDERS. Virginia: Time-Life Books, 1981
Angelucci, Enzo, World Encyclopedia OF CIVIL AIRCRAFT. New York: Crown, 1982
Bainbridge, Gordon E., THE OLD RHINEBECK AERODROME. New York: Exposition Press, 1977
Carpenter, Dorr B., and Mitch Mayborn, RYAN GUIDEBOOK. Texas: Flying Enterprizes, 1975
Casey, Louis S., CURTISS, THE HAMMONDSPORT ERA 1907-1915. New York: Crown, 1981
Casey, Louis S. and John Batchelor, NAVAL AIRCRAFT 1939-1945. Phoebus, 1975
Chant, Chris, WORLD WAR II AIRCRAFT. London: Orbis, 1975
Christy, Joe and Page Shamburger, COMMAND THE HORIZON. New York: Castle (A.S. Barnes) 1968
Davies, R.E.G., AIRLINES OF THE U.S. SINCE 1914. London: Putnam, 1972
Degner, Glenn and Lumen Winter, MINUTE EPICS OF FLIGHT. New York: Grosset and Dunlap, 1933
East, Omega G., WRIGHT BROTHERS NATIONAL MEMORIAL. Washington D.C.: U.S. Dept. of Interior, 1961
Feist, Uwe and Edward T. Maloney, CHANCE VOUGHT CORSAIR. California: Aero, 1967
Gilbert, James, THE WORLD'S WORST AIRCRAFT. New York: St. Martin's Press, 1976
Green, William and Gerald Pollinger, THE AIRCRAFT OF THE WORLD. New York: Hanover House, 1954
Hansen, Zenon, THE GOODYEAR AIRSHIPS. Illinois: Airship International Press, 1977
Hook, Thom, SHENANDOAH SAGA. Maryland: Air Show Publishers, 1973
Ingells, Douglas J., THE PLANE THAT CHANGED THE WORLD. California: Aero, 1966
Jablonski, Edward, AMERICA IN THE AIR WAR. Virginia: Time-Life Books, 1982
Jablonski, Edward, SEA WINGS. New York: Doubleday & Co. Inc., 1972
Jackson, Donald Dale, FLYING THE MAIL. Virginia: Time-Life Books, 1982
Jones, Lloyd S., U.S. FIGHTERS. California: Aero, 1975
Juptner, Joseph P., U.S. CIVIL AIRCRAFT VOLUMES #1 through #9. California: Aero, 1962 through 1981
Kurt, Franklin T. and Wolfgang Langewiesche, WATER FLYING. New York: Macmillan, 1974
Lambermont, Paul and Anthony Pirie, HELICOPTERS AND AUTOGYROS OF THE WORLD. New Jersey: A.S. Barnes, 1970
Matt, Paul R. HISTORICAL AVIATION ALBUM-VOLUMES #1, 2 and 5. California: Paul R. Matt, 1965-7
Mayborn, Mitch, GRUMMAN GUIDEBOOK. Texas: Flying Enterprizes, 1976
Mitchell, Kent A., THE SAGA OF THE FAIRCHILD AT-21. California: American Aviation Historical Society Journal, Vol. 32, #3, 1987
Morgan, Len, AIRLINERS OF THE WORLD. New York: Arco, 1966
Morgan, Len and R.P. Shannon, THE PLANES THE ACES FLEW-VOL. #3. Texas: Morgan Aviation Books, 1964
Morgan, Terry, THE LOCKHEED CONSTELLATION. New York: Arco, 1967
Munson, Kenneth and Gordon Swanborough, BOEING, AN AIRCRAFT ALBUM No. 4. New York: Arco, 1972
O'Neil, Paul, BARNSTORMERS AND SPEED KINGS. Virginia: Time-Life, 1981
Roseberry, C.R., THE CHALLENGING SKIES. New York: Doubleday, 1966
Smith, Frank Kingston, LEGACY OF WINGS. New York: Jason Aronson, 1981
Vorderman, Don, THE GREAT AIR RACES. New York: Doubleday, 1969
Young, Rosamond, TWELVE SECONDS TO THE MOON. Ohio: The Journal Herald, 1978